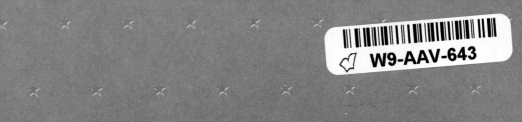

ess: an unforeseen meeting, an unanticipated result.

CHANCE ENCOUNTERS

True Stories of Unforeseen Meetings,
with Unanticipated Results

A. C. Greene

bright sky press

Albany, Texas and New York, New York

Also by A. C. Greene

$\mathcal{T}$o the luckiest chance encounter
I have experienced, that winter afternoon
when my late wife Betty introduced me to
a gorgeous brunette, saying, "This is Judy."
And, twenty-three years later, this encounter
which began by chance ended
permanently by design.

bright sky press

Albany, Texas/New York, New York

CHANCE ENCOUNTERS

EDITED BY: Fran Vick

DESIGNED BY: Tina Taylor, T2 Design

Copyright © 2002 by A. C. Greene

Manufactured in the United States of America

All rights reserved

Printed in the United States of America

10 9 8 7 6 5 4 3 2 1

Library of Congress Cataloging-in Publication Data

Greene, A. C., 1923- Chance encounters :
true stories of unforeseen meetings,with unanticipated results /
A.C. Greene.— 1st ed.

p. cm.

Includes index.

ISBN 0-9709987-9-1 (alk. paper)

1. Greene, A. C., 1923-
2. Greene, A. C., 1923—Friends and associates.
3. Authors, American—20th century—Biography.
4. Journalists—United States—Biography.
5. Texas—Biography.   I. Title.

PS3557.R3795 Z469 2002

814'.54—dc21   2001049950

Contents

Chance Encounters in the 1960s

Contents [continued]

Introduction

The defining nature of a chance encounter is unexpectedness: an unforeseen meeting, an unanticipated result. All of us have had chance encounters that dictated our future. Think how you met your husband or your wife, or perhaps how your mother and father met.

Historically, chance encounters have led to dramatic changes. General Benedict Arnold meets beautiful Peggy Shippen, and circumstances for the most infamous betrayal in American history begin. The Prince of Wales at a party encounters an American socialite, Mrs. Wallis Simpson, and the British throne rocks.

The State of Texas came about through a chance encounter. Moses Austin, of Missouri, was walking despondently across a windy, wintry plaza in San Antonio after having had his colonization proposal for Texas bluntly turned down by the Spanish governor. There Moses was, hundreds of wild and primitive miles from his home, a stranger in a strange town, discouraged and freezing, when, by chance, he encountered Felipe Enrique Neri, the self-styled Baron de Bastrop, whom he had met, briefly, in New Orleans nineteen years before and hadn't seen or heard of since. He had no idea the Baron was living in San Antonio—scarcely the place for a baron, self-styled or not.

Bastrop, though something of a scoundrel, was well respected by the Spanish. He invited Moses Austin to have a warming drink, heard out the Missourian's despair and within a few days had seen to it that Moses Austin's colonization plan was endorsed by the governor and on its way to higher Spanish authorities. Moses Austin returned home elated, but the cold, dangerous return journey proved fatal. He died within a few weeks, on his deathbed turning his "Texas Venture" over to his son, Stephen F. Austin. Stephen became the "Father of Texas"—because of a chance encounter.

★ ★ ★

The stories in this book are about chance encounters I have had over the years. These are true stories, although, like life, there is no theme to them. I was present for them for whatever reason: call it fate or the play of circumstances. Being a newspaper reporter helped, but not all my chance encounters came from newspaper days. Even when meeting certain people was part of my job, the outcome was not planned, and if I started out with a plan, there was an unlooked for outcome: I go to sell Coca Cola one night and almost begin a stage career; I walk into a West Texas movie house and end up sharing popcorn with Natalie Wood and Robert Wagner on their honeymoon; when our federal beat man is stricken with appendicitis, I am forced to cover a federal trial—and get thrown out of court.

What is unusual about many of these chance encounters is that they happened in unexpected places and involved unexpected people. Ronald Reagan in Abilene, Texas? Roy Rogers and I in South Philadelphia?

The idea that I was involved in these encounters might also be called unexpected. Other than service with the Marines in World War II, I have not had a romantic, wandering life around the globe, meeting kings and potentates. In fact, where could you have expected to have fewer chance encounters with fame or other vices than in small-town Texas? Only one set of my chance encounters took place under historical circumstances—these with various participants when I was a Dallas newspaper editor during the drama surrounding President John F. Kennedy's assassination.

Not all my chance encounters have been brief and of one-time quality. They may have all started that way, but now and then a bond has been created. But, without wanting to sound portentous, I feel there must be destiny in meetings which have such unforseen results. Some experiences are too rare not to be fated. We meet people we admire, people far outside our normal walk of life, and have no expectation of meeting again. And generally don't. But then, maybe on one side only of the meeting, a lifelong perception is gained or altered, a turn in the road is opened, a new planet is discovered for us—by a chance encounter.

This collection of stories represents chance encounters of the veriest kind. There is no continuity except that they happened to me. These are not the recollections of a man of the world or a public personality for whom such encounters are anything but chance. These are the encounters of a boy in a small Texas town, then a young man in that same town, then a newspaper editor who happened to be in a unique position to observe and participate in a rapidly changing world. There were few prearranged meetings or scheduled appearances on my part. I say all this so as to emphasize that these are truly encounters that took place by chance. Are they important? None of them is change-making except for me, and here I must admit, they have been of enormous change.

Some of these chance encounters have remained mileposts in my life: meeting and being with T. S. Eliot, getting to know and becoming friends with Artie Shaw and Stanley Marcus, photographing Franklin D. Roosevelt—events and celebrations with which I can, at this later date, find nothing but joy and thankfulness for their having taken place.

But isn't life a series of chance encounters? Not for royalty, perhaps, but for the rest of us: I am seated in a classroom of a university in which I am not enrolled, taking a night class. In walks a lovely girl I had never seen before and who, had I not needed three advanced university hours, I would never have met. She was engaged when I met her, but three years later, after having met her again by chance, I married her. But readers can supply a hundred such personal instances.

I suppose these chance encounters have become more possible in recent years. Television, E-mail, the Internet, all make such encounters more common. But regardless, my own chance encounters are not from persistence, or from shrewd perception, or skill at the computer, they are merely—as I look back over the hundreds of opportunities for things to have gone completely otherwise—by chance.

Chance Encounters
in the 1930s–1940s

Jarmila Novotna

Young A.C. Greene.
A confident politician at age 12.

Swinging the Texas Vote

$\mathcal{M}$y first encounter with fame came when I was eleven years old. It was 1936 and Democrat Franklin D. Roosevelt was running for a second term. His Republican opponent was Alf Landon. I was for neither. Always backing the underdog—even then I was a St. Louis Browns fan—my support went to William Lemke, a North Dakota congressman and the Union Party candidate. I knew nothing of the Union Party or Lemke's platform—or Lemke, for that matter. I thought his name was "Lempke." My sympathies went to him because his task was so hopeless.

A prime news magazine at the time was *The Literary Digest* to which my grandmother subscribed. One popular achievement of *The Literary Digest* was its national "Straw Poll." Included in each magazine was a card which could be filled out and mailed in with the reader's choice of presidential candidates. I was thumbing through the magazine, which was not the kind that eleven-year-olds usually thumb through, when I encountered the "Straw Poll" card. I gazed in wonder and, as old comic strips used to depict, a light bulb lighted above my head. Here was a chance, my chance, to strike a blow for the underdog. Without telling anyone what I had in mind, I began gently pillaging friendly subscribers' copies of *The Literary Digest* and rummaging through neighborhood trash bins seeking discarded magazines. I eventually accumulated a dozen "Straw Poll" cards, and somehow, in my

Depression-riddled piggy bank, I accumulated the twelve cents needed for postage. Signing different names, I voted for "William Lemke" on all twelve cards, although, as mentioned, misspelling the name. On one card I composed a short poem which began, "Though he's not a local resident/Let's make Lempke [sic] President!"

During that fall a radio news program broadcast the results of this national straw vote. William Lemke was seldom mentioned. I waited intently for next week's "Straw Poll" broadcast. It began with the usual statistics: FDR was trouncing Alf Landon by the same straw landslide the actual balloting later produced. I was sick that no mention was made of William Lemke's standing. But suddenly the radio announcer added, "And we have a political phenomenon. From little ol' Abilene, Texas come twelve votes for William Lemke. Possibly the farm vote? One ardent supporter even included a heartfelt poem about his candidate."

Fame struck this eleven-year-old from little ol' Abilene, Texas hard. Even though I didn't dare admit to my family what I had done, I felt I had swung the whole state to Lemke. I was a political genius. My delight was topped out a night later when Frank Smith, a lawyer and local Democratic politician—all politicians in our town were Democrats—told my dad that after hearing the "Straw Poll" broadcast, he'd spent a couple of hours in the courthouse futilely seeking names of registered Union Party voters. At that point I dreamed of marching boldly into the polling place to announce I represented a dozen votes for William Lemke. It only occurred to me on Election Day that I was not only taking my triumph in the "Straw Poll" too literally but—political genius or not—I was too young to vote.

The Opera Singer In the Red Dress

*A*ge fourteen used to be (and may be still) a terrible age to be a boy. You know you're a man, inside, but outside you're a kid with pimples, or a lovely boy soprano whose voice has cracked but still lingers between male and female. You're lonely. You're afraid to admit it. The girls you've known all your life have suddenly become women, dating grown men of sixteen or seventeen and (you perceive) harboring an especial dislike for fourteen-year-old males. You can hardly wait to get your revenge, but (of course) when the time comes and you are sixteen or seventeen, you've forgotten who you wanted to get revenge on, you're so entranced by a new crop of fourteen- and fifteen-year-old girls.

Midway in my fourteenth year I was developing, carefully (and with study and effort), personal dignity, assuring myself I was superior to other fourteen-year-old boys. I also elaborated a calm interior plan which I felt gave me more self-assurance than those others. For one thing I began to wear a necktie to school and I was furious if my mother made me wear shirts on which she had "turned the collar"—a process unknown today, involving the frugal mother carefully ripping off the frayed collar, then turning the worn collar over and resewing the unfrayed side to the shirt.

At this period of precarious manhood, I obtained a ticket to a concert by the esteemed opera singer, Madame Jarmila Novotna. I must have found it because I know I couldn't come up with the required fifty cents for a student ticket singlehandedly. I decided this concert would be a suitable launching pad for my new self-recognition of dignity and assurance. The city's adult elite would be there, not a bunch of immature high school sophomores to mar the evening.

I wasn't altogether familiar with opera music, although I knew I was no philistine—a satisfying word whose non-Biblical use I had just learned.

I told my parents I was going to hear an opera singer in concert at the high school. My dad raised an eyebrow at my coat and tie and said to Mother, "Is our son suddenly becoming a man?" and to me, "Do you have a date?" Horrified (or terrified) that they should think that, I vigorously denied having even the thought of taking some silly girl. Neither of my parents objected that I was going out alone at night. We only lived six blocks from the school, and in those days in our town boys (or girls, for that matter) never thought of being mugged or knifed or shot from some passing automobile. And with my adult poise, I was past having to be told when to come in.

At the concert hall (the same high school auditorium where I attended assembly three times a week) I was given a program and ushered to my seat. Suddenly the ordinary auditorium became a Broadway theater, the shadows, the faces, the low murmur of the audience, all making my spirit giddy. I noticed that several of the men were wearing tuxedos. When the concert began, Madame Novotna swept onstage in a flaming red sheath gown, bowing and smiling. Her singing was wonderful. I heard a woman behind me telling her husband that Madame Novotna "is a true diva." At the intermission curtain several men stood shouting, "Brava!" as they applauded her off the stage. I vowed that if the men stood and shouted "Brava!" again, I would stand and shout with them.

Well, the concert continued at the same high level of excitement. At the final curtain, after suitable encores, the men stood again, applauding and shouting "Brava!" but I decided I would wait for another concert to do that. Possibly when I had a tuxedo, which I vowed I would buy with the first twenty-five dollars I earned. However, tuxedo or not, I told myself I was mature enough to be a true fan. I would go backstage and ask the opera star for her autograph. It was a pretty daring decision. I hoped she could tell I had already begun to shave.

Feeling very adult, I rehearsed a little speech as I went: "Madame Novotna, I wanted to stand and holler 'Brava!' after every bar you sang!" I found the stage door and mounted the short stairs to the right wings. There she was, in her bright red dress, talking with two men—in tuxedos, of course. I waited nervously for the men to leave, and as they walked away I went to her and thrust my program toward her, completely unable to remember my rehearsed speech, saying simply, "Would you mind signing this?"

She looked at me with a slight smile, then said, "Why, certainly not." She scribbled her name and I, with fervent thanks, left the stage on wings of song, so to speak. Clutching the precious document to my bosom, I hurried through the auditorium out to the lighted vestibule and being careful I was not observed, took out the program and read, "To a boy and his program" signed, "Mrs. Norvell Howell."

The red dress had fooled me. Cursing my immaturity, I fled into the night.

It was twenty-five years before I again asked for an autograph.

*Bill Mauldin,
war cartoonist and
writer, at his desk.*

The Army Comes to Abilene

In 1940 the town of Abilene was famous within Texas for being pious—a sort of "holy city." It had three church-related institutions of higher learning, was bone dry, didn't allow dancing in the public schools—no sock-hops, no Junior or Senior Proms—and within certain denominational confines, offered a church of your choice within walking distance of home. When you moved to Abilene the first two questions you were asked were: what church do you folks go to? and, are you a Democrat? You could answer the first question with any name you liked, but you'd better not say "None." That might haunt you at the bank when you applied for a loan. And if you weren't a Democrat, best not make too big a deal of being a Republican. Abilene was a quiet place, not much crime—couple of bootleggers, a stolen car now and then, a mama-and-daddy disturbance—but no dope, no drive-by shootings, no major frauds or scandals involving the police, the sheriff's office or the city administration.

Then, in December of 1940, the whole picture began changing. That was when the Chamber of Commerce proudly announced that through its herculean efforts, Abilene had been named the site for the United States Army's Camp Barkeley, bringing in thousands of men and women to a region where the Depression was still more fact than memory. Within two months the tent city camp was officially opened, mud and all, and the 45th (Thunderbird) Division had started moving in. The Thunderbird was a fortunate choice for Texas duty because it consisted of National Guard units from familiar neighboring states: Oklahoma, New Mexico, Colorado and Arizona.

With the bombing of Pearl Harbor, Camp Barkeley expanded immensely and by the summer of 1942 what had been a tent city was being converted, three tents at a time, to structures called "hutments." I went to work for the enviable wage of forty cents an hour, time-and-a-half overtime and double-time on Sundays. I held the lowliest position in the construction chain, my job being, in carpenters' lingo, "pissanting" lumber—fetching and keeping the carpenters supplied with whatever cut or size of board was needed. Every worker, even pissants, had to join the Carpenters and Joiners Union, per government regulations. Forced membership didn't bother me the way it did some of the workers brought up on Texas' traditional anti-union sentiments. My Grandfather George, a master carpenter and cabinet maker, had been a strong union supporter.

I soon discovered that if I wanted to explore a bit all I had to do was hoist a couple of two-by-fours on my shoulder and walk around looking busy, although the carpenters were fond of scornfully urging the helpers to hurry up: "Dollar waitin' on a dime!" It was a fairly simple task to keep my team of carpenters supplied with enough boards—each structure used the same numbers and cuts—so every now and again I would stroll about seeing what went on.

Several times I noticed one soldier, who looked about age fifteen, seated at the outdoor swimming pool. One day he gave me a friendly nod and I put down my two-bys briefly and joined him. I asked him what he did that got him off the drill field. He laughed and said, "I have a good job, but it doesn't get me out of drill." He said he was with the *45th Division News*.

I thought perhaps I'd be a newspaperman when the war was over. I asked him if he was a reporter and he said, "I'm the staff cartoonist. If I'm lucky, once I draw my daily cartoon, and do a few little dingbats, I'm free for a while." His name was Bill Mauldin and he was born in New Mexico and had gone to school in Arizona. He'd recently married an Abilene girl named Norma Jean. We chatted several more times after that first meeting.

The 45th Division went overseas not long after I met him and Bill Mauldin became a cartoonist with *Stars & Stripes*, the army newspaper. He won the Pulitzer Prize for cartooning in 1944 and eventually wrote five war-time books, including the bestseller, *Up Front with Mauldin*. At war's end he was the most celebrated cartoonist in American, a distinction he held for decades.

I never met Bill Mauldin again, but I have one of his original editorial cartoons, inscribed, hanging in my sitting room. It was done in 1961 while he was with the St. Louis *Post-Dispatch*. My wife Judy's father, the late John M. Dalton, had just been sworn in as Governor of Missouri and Mauldin depicted him with sleeve rolled up, a scantling in hand, facing a stubborn Missouri Mule.

You never know, do you, when or how your path may again cross someone's with whom, years before, you had a mere chance encounter? Time teaches us patience.

Backstage Character: Me

After Camp Barkeley was opened, the military quickly permeated every aspect of the town of Abilene, whose 27,000 population was dramatically enhanced by the sudden infusion of soldiers, families and followers. Then, early in 1942, a Medical Replacement Training Center opened which added thousands of MDs and other medical personnel to Barkeley. At a concert by the Boston Pops at Hardin-Simmons University, a woman fainted during intermission and some civic worthy brought out a microphone and pleaded, "Is there a doctor in the house?" It was a grand sight as more than fifty uniformed physicians stood and started toward the front. In their honor the Boston Pops played "Deep in the Heart of Texas," with the audience, under the baton of conductor Arthur Fiedler, joining in the rhythmic handclapping.

In the spring of 1943 I had already enlisted in the Navy and was waiting to be called to active duty. Since my college classes were on an iffy basis—I never knew when the Navy would call me—I worked for the Texas Coca Cola Bottling Co. of Abilene which was bottling twenty-four hours a day. I had worked there before and knew plant operation, and since a good many operators had been drafted, the company was glad to have me on any basis, so I worked pretty much my own hours, just so I was present at the intervals when the line was shut down for cleaning and greasing. This round-the-clock, full speed production schedule was making the outdated machinery—the old clutch-and-brake Myers-Dumore soaker (the bottle washer and sterilizer) and the liquid carbonation and crown (capper) machinery—cry for pity, not to mention the strain put on those humans at the end of the bottling line who filled cases and six-packs by hand. (Fortunately, we only used the famous six-ounce hobble-skirt bottles.)

One night Nib Shaw, the plant manager, called me to ask if I would work overtime. The Mills box (a type of coin machine) backstage at Camp Barkeley's main theater had quit taking nickels and he didn't have time to send somebody to fix it. He gave me the key to the box and asked me to go there and take nickels by hand and serve cold Cokes the same way. When I first worked for Coca Cola (pre-war)

Ann Sothern

you could imperil your job calling it "Coke." It was feared "Coke" implied cocaine.

"And don't make change for people who want to use it for the Dr Pepper machine." At that time none of the coin machines made change. Mr. Shaw, father of one of my grade school friends, said there was going to be a big crowd. The attraction was a roadshow performance of that wild circus of a theater piece, *Hellzapoppin* with Olson and Johnson. Although there was a commercial pass on the pick-up, I had no trouble getting through the post's main gate without a personal pass. Wearing a Coca Cola uniform, which included both a visored cap and a black leather bow-tie, seems to be all the pass I needed. I used to wonder why the FBI or CIA or the Texas Rangers didn't use a Coca Cola uniform to get into well guarded outlaw establishments. In 1947, as a Coca Cola driver in Dallas, I walked in the back door of many a notorious gambling lair, past tough, pistol packin' guards who were holding huge Doberman pinchers quiescent, as I delivered cases of Coke.

Backstage at the Camp Barkeley theater I found the Mills machine, with half a dozen impatient actors and stagehands surrounding it. The bottling plant office had been closed and I was unable to get the five bucks worth of change I had planned on. I unlocked the machine and found less than two dollars in the coin box, and the first person in line offered me a five-dollar bill. My predicament was somewhat relieved when the big spender sneered he only wanted change to buy a Dr Pepper anyway.

Appearing along with *Hellzapoppin'* was actress Ann Sothern, the buxom film idol who, by the time I arrived at the theater, already had the military audience ready to charge the stage. She came back to me, shaking her head and asking, "Can you give me a Coke on credit? I don't want to have to go get my purse from the dressing room." I said credit was no problem, in fact, I said I'd give her one on the house, and short-change somebody if I had to.

"By golly, you're a man after my own heart," she said, which I found a singularly appropriate remark for her to make, seeing that at the most significant plant on the bosom of her tight fitting gown a four-inch heart-shaped piece had been cut from the fabric, although I was afraid to glance, afraid it would turn into a stare! I was only nineteen—she was a lady of twenty-nine. I hadn't known Ann Sothern was going to be at Camp Barkeley, but once I discovered that *there she was* the ten years was no barrier to my youthful appetite. One thing about movies—they made it o.k. for us teen age boys to lust after women who (in some cases) were old enough to be our mothers.

Miss Sothern returned to my little place of backstage business several times, once dragging a chair out of a nearby room and sitting with me for a short period, although most of the time she was surrounded by members of the cast or stagehands. She was tough but good natured. She claimed she was actually a country girl, despite the dozens of sophisticated roles she had played, born in North Dakota and raised in Iowa. I asked her about "Sothern" and she said her real name was Harriette Lake. She had a sister, Bonnie Lake, who sang with some of the "big bands." I said I found Lake a pretty name, why didn't she keep it, but she said, "You don't argue with the studio. I'd have gone with 'Maude' if they'd said do it or else." My grandmother Maude was my favorite person on earth, but I recognized the antique quality of her name.

The stage production of *Hellzapoppin'* was one of those Broadway successes with very little plot line, and a varying one at that. Actors jump up from the audience doing and saying ridiculous things or came strolling down the aisle making ridiculous puns. (Example: two men emerge from a stage door carrying a long ladder. When asked, from the stage, what in the world they are doing, one of them replies, "We heard the drinks are on the house.")

I only peeked out front now and then if a louder than usual burst of laughter took place. My time was fully occupied with Miss Sothern and the other thirsty actors. But the fact I had on a Coca Cola uniform caused many of the stage people to think I was part of the show. One asked, rather peevishly I thought, "When are you going to go on? Every time I come back here, there you sit." Ann Sothern said if I went walking across the stage in my uniform nobody would blink an eye probably—"just ad lib something clever." In that case, I might do the same thing, I said.

"Hey, do it," she urged. "Just stroll out there like you're part of the show. See what happens. If anybody gets horsey I'll protect you."

I said I had to dispense cold Coca Cola, but Ann Sothern laughed,

"I'll handle your job for you—if you trust me."

I stood there torn between fear and fame.

"Go on," she whispered, giving me the gentlest sort of push. I took several brave steps toward the wings and got to the right entrance, with Miss Sothern urging, "Go on . . . you can make it." But one glimpse of the stage itself, and I panicked. A very sharp-eyed member of the audience, positioned in just the right seat and staring at just the right spot, might have seen a blur and thought someone had missed an entrance cue. I hurried back to the safety of my Coca Cola machine—and to the disapproval of Ann Sothern.

A thousand times since, I've wished I'd tried it.

Roy Rogers and a Snap of a Trigger

$\mathcal{N}$ot all my chance encounters with musical fame took place in West Texas. When I was an impromptu photographer at the Philadelphia Naval Hospital in World War II, I served as the unlooked for picture taker for Roy Rogers. He and his horse Trigger and a group of back-up singers, guitar players and an accordionist, were down from New York on a quick visit to the hospital and a couple of other sites in Philadelphia. When he arrived I got several shots of Roy Rogers for use in the next issue of the station newspaper, of which I was editor.

Roy's performance took place outdoors and after he had done some singing plus tricks aboard Trigger, he was swarmed by sailors (and Waves) trying to get his autograph. He never said no to the patients, and I think he would have ridden Trigger right onto the bedfast wards if someone had desired him to. (The elevators, built to handle stretchers and or carts, were big enough to handle Trigger.) I got more photos and was standing by when one of the back-up singers, also standing by, asked me if he could get a print of a shot he had been in. I said I thought so and he gave me his card. I looked at the name, Al Rinehart, and asked, "Aren't you from Texas? Didn't you used to sing with the Universal Cowboys?" Well, he was from Texas, West Texas, as a matter of fact—San Angelo—and he had led the Universal (a brand of flour) Cowboys. We immediately began a conversation about Texas musicians. Al had played with the Lightcrust Doughboys at one point, knew Bob Wills and his "Texas Playboys," and was familiar with Pappy W. Lee O'Daniel, the former Texas Governor, now in 1944, Senator, who had started out as leader of the Lightcrust Doughboys, then had formed his own hillbilly band advertising his own Hillbilly brand flour.

Al told me, "We've been traveling so far and so fast that I haven't heard a West Texas voice in months." I asked him if Roy Rogers didn't carry his own photographer and P.R. man, but Rinehart said the visit to Philadelphia had been hastily made up without the usual ensemble. "This trip it's just us and Trigger."

Rinehart introduced me to Roy Rogers and suggested the cowboy singer might like some of my pictures. I said certainly. Rogers seemed genuinely delighted. He asked, "Why don't you go along with us the rest of th' day and shoot pictures?" I said, "Roy, I'd love to do it, but I'm just an enlisted men." Roy grinned and said, "I think I can take care of that." To make a long story short, when Roy Rogers asked permission to use me for a day, the request might as well have come from the Fleet Admiral, so quick was the affirmative response. In addition, that afternoon both the *Philadelphia Inquirer* and the tabloid *Daily News* asked the Navy permission to use pictures I had taken— the ranks of their photography staffs depleted by the draft and they'd not assigned anyone to cover Roy Rogers's unscheduled visit.

I thoroughly enjoyed the brief tour of duty that Roy Rogers, his company and I, made. He was a most accommodating celebrity, and celebrity he was, being recognized on sight by everyone on the streets. The Philadelphia Naval Hospital is far down in South Philly, below the section then known as "Little Italy" (the first place I ever ate pizza). I figured if there was a locale where Roy Rogers would not be recognized it would be Little Italy, but I was wrong. When we rode up Broad Street in an open car, Rogers splendid in his glittering western attire (and I in the front seat, with camera) people at the

(From left to right) Al Rinehart, Roy Rogers and back up singer.

curb or on the sidewalk began waving and exclaiming, "Roy! Roy!" and there was one Broad Street intersection where we stopped for a traffic light and the car was swarmed with autograph seekers. If a police escort hadn't arrived, we might have had to spend the day right there, Roy was so obliging to his fans.

Several times that day, as I was shooting pictures, I was asked for my autograph and once was accused of being Red Skelton in disguise. "Com' on, Red . . . you're not in th' Navy." I went into my best, "Aw, shucks" routine when I denied it, probably hoping, in my sneaky heart, the man didn't believe me. I told my little fan club that I had been assigned by the Navy to cover Roy Rogers' visit. After the first couple of requests, I began signing my name "Ace" Greene. I felt modestly heroic, and heroically modest.

Rogers was courteous and kindly disposed to the crowds that

sometimes pushed courtesy to the edge. He kept on smiling and never, in my presence at least, did anything to blemish his "yes, ma'am," sort of reputation. Although born in Cincinnati, Ohio, I thought he acted more like a native-born Texan. He even thanked me for "taking the time" to go with them.

As usual in my chance encounters, I didn't meet Roy Rogers again, but I always felt close to him. In 1946 his first wife died, then he married Dale Evans, a Texas native. Dale began her singing career on a Dallas radio show called "The Early Birds" which got me (and thousands of others) started each morning. I still have some of the pictures I took of Roy Rogers in Philadelphia. They're pretty darn good, if "Ace" Greene says so himself.

A Bit of Foreign Duty

*N*owadays they don't ask us old World War II warriors, "What did you do in the war?" like they used to. Nowadays they don't know there was a war before Vietnam. But when they do ask me about "my war" I give them a matter-of-fact look in the eye and say, "I ran a Chinese whorehouse for the U. S. Navy." I don't defend it. I know I'm going to have to go through a few outraged comments about how morally depraved this was, both from the standpoint of the ethnic Chinese and the abuse of females. And I agree. But I also point out that it happened to me by chance, that I was ordered on the job by a very high ranking Navy officer—and the whorehouse itself had been established before the Navy landed.

Once or twice I have had some younger person ask me if a whore was anything like a prostitute. Apparently prostitute is a more sympathetic title than whore, which, I'll admit, has a terribly old fashioned sound. And sometimes, believe it or not, someone asks me what a whorehouse is. One or two women have asked, without trying to be humorous, what I do for a living now. But by greater odds, I get called a liar, and sometimes an old hand will add that I am a traitor to the U. S. Navy or the Marine Corps, even by telling such a tale, true or not.

Here's what happened. I was a Navy Medical Corpsman—Pharmacist Mate 3rd Class—attached to the U. S. Marines. The Marines do not have their own medical corps, and the title of Pharmacist Mate is not to be misconstrued: it is (or was) merely a Navy rating and has nothing to do with a drug store.

I was satisfied, under the circumstances, with my situation following the Japanese surrender in 1945. The Sixth Marine Division, of which I was a part, had been sent up from Guam to Tsingtao (now Qingdao), in Shantung Province, China, to accept the surrender of several thousand Japanese troops still under arms. Tsingtao was a large city and my unit was stationed at the old German Army's Moltke Compound—leftover evidence of 1899–1914 when Tsingtao was under German control. At one end of the compound was a brewery, built by the Germans, where delicious Asahi beer was produced—a liter bottle for ten cents! (Now sold as "Tsingtao Beer," China's finest brew.)

With the war over and the point system in operation—in which time overseas counted toward getting back to the states—most of the old "rock happy" Marines had been sent home. Thus, because there

Bottom left, A.C. Greene aboard a rickshaw. Right, fellow Marines posed at the famous "First Class Brothel" in Tsingtao, China.

were so few higher rating non-coms left, I was cozily heading up a little "kingdom." I was the Regimental Medical Records clerk and had my own office (where I also lived) in dark and Germanic old Moltke Barracks. A Navy medical doctor was in charge of medical operations, but he was fresh from the States, was seldom needed in Sick Bay (the Navy version of an Emergency Ward), and left things pretty much up to us corpsmen while he and two other bachelor M.D.'s had a downtown apartment shared by (it was said) a number of lovely White Russian ladies.

We Guam Marines had been in Tsingtao about ten days when I got a 6 A.M. call on the field telephone from a brisk lieutenant j.g. USNR from the Division Surgeon's office. He asked if this was H&S Battery, 15th Marines, and I replied yes, and after a moment's thought added, "Sir."

The brisk lieutenant j.g. then said that on orders of the Division Surgeon, I was to make up a detail and report before noon to some utterly unrepeatable Chinese address. When I showed dullness at the location he broke the officer-enlisted man barrier (after all, the war was over) long enough to say in a mild, whiny voice, "Oh, you know, Pee Hei Loony's Reno Square."

Even with less than a fortnight ashore, there was scarcely a Marine or sailor in Tsingtao who didn't know where Reno Square was.

"But lieutenant, that's a whorehouse," I hollered over the field telephone. "What do they want with us in a whorehouse?"

The headquarters j.g. gave me a motherly chuckle. "We want you to set up a pro station and a duty roster to oversee its operation."

I protested that I was the Regimental Medical Records clerk, not part of the sick-bay watch, but to no avail. I just happened to be the corpsman who answered the phone.

A pro station (prophylactic station) was supplied with what were called pro kits. No use going into details, but the pro kit contained a tube of disease killer with a small point on it. You must also understand, in this age of AIDS and other terrible epidemics, that during World War II nothing was so dreaded as syphilis. The Navy even had special toilets marked "Leutic" for syphilitics to use—although in three years of Navy duty, I never saw anyone use one. I think the marked toilet, like the word leutic itself, was a holdover from the old pre-war Navy when the infected were treated with arsenicals, bismuth or mercurials. But by 1945 even the Navy was treating syphilis with penicillin.

At any rate, when the j.g. said I should set up a pro station, gall filled my existence. Running a pro station was for stateside. When you got overseas, let the damned Marines look out for their own romantic welfare. Besides, I was no "chancre mechanic." I didn't treat venereal disease. I said as much to the Navy j.g. He let me expel my gripe, then told me what he termed, "a mitigating circumstance": Reno Square henceforth was to be "Officer Country." No enlisted men allowed. Surely I wouldn't mind duty with officers and gentlemen? He added that the Division Surgeon had personally suggested we get underway with the project at once—as if that should give me brownie points—and rang off.

I began rounding up a couple of fellow corpsmen to assist in guarding the vitals of the officers of the U. S. Navy and Marine Corps. We piled a jeep with pans, a kerosene stove, a folding OR table and half a gross of pro kits. Reno Square was located in the heart of Tsingtao's "native" district. The formidable stucco building, looming over the gloomy street, was three stories high and built on the order of a traditional Mexican house, with a high arched entrance leading to an interior patio with balconies encircling all but the bottom floor.

We entered the place somewhat gingerly. We were met by a Chinaman who couldn't have been anymore Hollywood if he had ushered at Grauman's Chinese Theater. Hands tucked into the wide sleeves of his black coat, he bowed and looked quizzically at us. We looked quizzically at him.

"You want gurrs?" he asked.

I went into a chopped up sign language cum pidgin English to try and explain our mission, but my message got nowhere with the Grauman usher, whom I decided was the proprietor (in pure phonetics), Mr. Pee Hei Loony. Only after he had called in half a dozen others, one of whom kept asking, "gentaman so-gers seek preasure?" did we establish a beachhead. I presumed it was a beachhead because after I had explained we weren't seeking pleasure but were there "on business," Pee Hei Loony stepped aside to let "Seek Preasure?" guide us farther into the interior.

"Seek Preasure?" showed us a small room which looked onto the patio. Through all the Boy Scout American Indian signs we could muster, we were shown the water supply and were taken on a tour of the establishment. One of the corpsmen with me, a short, blond boy from Indianapolis, still in his teens, casually opened a door and withdrew in amazement: "There's a naked girl in there!" he shouted. I briefed him on the purpose of this Chinese House of Flowers. From then on he led the way. I don't think we realized it but we were being offered a display of the merchandise for a sampling of our choice. (I am too upright to lie: I didn't sample a thing.)

The pro station was put into operation and among our early customers was a Navy Commander with nineteen months solid sea duty behind him (he said). He wore shoulder boards with three gold stripes and "scrambled eggs" on his cap visor. He spurned our offer of precautious solicitude and strode boldly into the courtyard. The descending darkness had brought out the inhabitants, along with what appeared to be a considerable passel of kinfolks. The girls were lined up along the railing of the balconies, chattering, laughing, yelling . . . a melodic, if off-key, bedlam.

The salty Commander turned to me, "Well, whadda I do now, corpsman?"

"Sir, if you don't know someone else will have to show you because I'm on duty."

The Commander patiently explained that he had to date invaded 827 such establishments on six of the seven continents and that he only wished to know the ground rules. One of my faults is I have never learned when to admit ignorance, and here I made a mistake. Instead of turning him over to Pee Hei Loony or ol' "Seek Preasure?" I pointed to a cluster of beauties leaning over the rail and said, "Take your pick Commander. They're all the same price." The officer stood making a happy inventory, turned and winked, and started toward the balcony of his choice.

Pee Hei Loony, standing at my elbow and looking inscrutably Chinese, saw me apparently giving orders to a great official. He must have decided that I was sent to assume command of his ship because from that moment he retired from active management of Reno

Square and watched me with wonder and love.

While my fellow corpsmen and I were trying to figure "where do we go from here?" a Naval aviator came down from the third floor and asked, with a lascivious grin, "You runnin' this lash-up?" I said I had only come aboard to set up a pro station.

"Well, how much do I owe?" I turned to "Seek Preasure?" and asked a question that seems to be easily understood anywhere on the globe: "How much?" He looked at me, bowed, and said graciously, "Yes." I repeated the question, he repeated the answer: "Yes."

I pondered a moment and remembered a popular novel by William Bradford Huie in which a Pearl Harbor brothel had advertised, "Three dollars for three minutes." The amount sounded reasonable to my inexperienced mind—the stipulated time having no relevance—so I said to the Navy flier, "That will be three dollars." The flier asked, "Three dollars American?" I said, "Of course. I don't think they print a Chinese bill lower than a thousand bucks."

The flier—he was an ensign—handed me a U. S. five dollar bill. I told him I didn't have change; we would have to ask the management. When I showed "Seek Preasure?" the bill he made another gracious comment, "Yes!" and hurried out and across the patio. Returning, he had an old fashioned wooden cigar box—one with a little brass catch on the lid—and handed it to me, saying, "Yes."

In it I found five one dollar bills, American. I gave the flier his change, pointed him to a pro kit, and despite his protests, made him use it. "This is embarrassing," he said, "I've never used one of these damn things." I said it was Navy regs and the Navy might take his airplane away from him if he refused—which was wholly my own interpretation. He stood, grinning, with the tube in his hand.

"I don't need this."

"Now, wouldn't you hate to take some loathsome disease home to your sweet wife?" I asked, trying my best to sound as unctuous as a chaplain's assistant.

"I ain't married," he said. But he used the prophylaxis with me observing. I didn't tell him it was a case of *voyeurism;* I'd never seen one used, either.

Back to the Commander: his engagement was brief and successful. He reported back to the quarterdeck less than fifteen minutes later, wadding Chinese money into my hand. I waved him to Pee Hei Loony. Pee Hei Loony bowed, smiled, and pointed him to me. I ended up taking $2,500 in Chinese money from the wad. (The exchange rate was 800 to 1, U. S.) Pee Hei Loony muttered in his wisp of beard the universal sign of Chinese approval, "Ding how."

Before I left we had several more customers and the Chinese management simply turned everything over to us, including the money. I don't know whether they trusted us or thought we were officially expropriating their operation. After all, Tsingtao had been under the rule of four different nations and no telling how many warlords within thirty-one years.

Next morning I called Division Headquarters to report the success of our excursion, and noted that we not only had set up the pro station but seemed to be running the whole shebang. That suited Headquarters; I was given a "Well done" and told that a Shore Patrol ensign and two helpers would be down to Pee Hei Loony's to screen candidates and make sure nothing but officers entered. (The S.P.s never showed up.)

Our take the first night, converting the U. S. dollars, had been about $33,000 in Chinese Federal Reserve Bank notes. As more and more U. S. military men began using Chinese money, I set an arbitrary scale of $2,500 FRBs per fifteen minutes or fraction thereof with the exchange rate at 800 to 1. But the exchange rate rose so quickly that within a month it had hit 3,000 to one and my fiscal projection was knocked silly. Which led to a most human episode: a young Marine lieutenant from an infantry regiment laughed, one night, "I can hardly wait to tell my grandchildren that granddaddy once paid 10,000 bucks for a piece of Chinese tail!" But he didn't get to boast: he was killed in a Jeep accident the next week.

Only one time did I accompany Pee Hei Loony and his business manager to buy new girls. I never went again. It was a shattering experience despite the fact that most of the girls were not only sold by their families but frequently brought their family along with them. The girls seemed to be regarded with honor because of the unusually high income they made for the family.

As word spread through the officers in Tsingtao that Reno Square was off limits to enlisted men our trade grew. We welcomed our first

U. S. general aboard two weeks after I became unofficial skipper. He asked my advice as to available billets and was so pleased with the results that he lamented the fact I was a Navy man and he, an Army one-star, couldn't promote me.

There was some difficulty at first in convincing the girls that we Corpsmen were not at Reno Square as clients. One in particular, her little round face glowing with love, followed me around saying over and over, "Tex! Tex!" (That was the name I had stenciled over the left hand pocket of my Marine Corp fatigue jacket: everybody from Texas, except Fleet Admiral Nimitz, was called "Tex.") I discovered the girl was losing face because her love was unrequited. Finally I told Pee Hei Loony to explain to the girls that the Marine Corps fed us enlisted men special powders to lessen our impulses so that we would do our job "with the greatest excellence." Chemical eunuchs, so to speak. He mulled this intelligence in his wispy chin and sadly shook his head, mumbling "boo how"—the opposite of "ding how."

There must have been a hundred different girls at Reno Square during the months we were there. We soon worked up a chatting arrangement with most of them. They were great teases and would gather on the balconies in front of their rooms and jeer and laugh at officers who, on entering the courtyard, showed shyness or hesitation to make a choice.

"Hey, Joe . . . you wanna leeta boy 'stead gurrl?"

The Chinese names were more than we could handle in the original, running mostly to such concoctions as Beautiful Mist, Peacock's Cry or Moon on the Mountain. To expedite matters we began calling them by the names of movie stars we fancied they resembled. My personal favorite was Hedy Lamar. She had been raised in a missionary's house and knew enough English to converse on cosmetics ("lipstick," however, was beyond her), baseball ("Bab Root"), and movies, unfortunately, silent pictures only. We had a slight bit of trouble applying the names of blonde actresses—all the Chinese girls had black hair—but we went more by preference than looks, so we had Betty Grable, June Haver and Gloria De Haven, as well as a raven-haired example titled Yvonne de Carlo.

Despite their "occupation," if you will, the Chinese girls were, in certain ways, innocent. They were reluctant to refer to sex, or sexual activity. I wondered that some of them didn't seem to realize what they were doing. Their attitude was certainly not in the manner of an American prostitute. Occasionally one of us would make some kind of sexual blunder trying to speak the Mandarin tonal dialect used in North China where we were. Once I pulled the hair on my forearm and pronounced it something like "pee-zhu." This provoked gales of laughter from some girls who informed me I was saying "beer." But later an English speaking Chinese friend told me they were laughing because I had used the tone that meant pubic hair. But ah, yes, say it slightly differently and it meant beer.

Like most Americans I believed that all Chinese were small. But one evening I was stunned to see a Chinese soldier enter the court-yard who towered more than seven feet high. He was wearing the blue cotton uniform of the Chinese communist Eighth Route Army, a red star on his cap. He was also wearing a big machine pistol whose wooden holster could be attached to make it a shoulder weapon. I looked around for Pee Hei Loony or "Seek Preasure?" but no male Chinese was in sight. I went out and sternly shook my head saying, "Mig-wa bing-ying" which means "American soldier," and tried every other way I knew to inform him this sporting arena was for officers and gentlemen, but he was unimpressed. He made a strong dismissive gesture with his left hand (which only missed me by a few inches) and I stepped aside.

Our encounter took place in utter silence, the girls watched without making a sound. Big Boy spotted one to his liking and pointed, shouting something in Chinese or Mongolian—I think he was Mongolian. His choice turned and ran into a room. He started after her and his machine pistol, slung carelessly at his side in the company of two potato-masher grenades, discouraged me from interfering further.

Moments later a wild cry shattered the enclosure and a half-dressed Marine Infantry lieutenant came tumbling down the stairs.

"My god, Fu Manchu just commandeered my room," he yelled, "why th' hell didn't you stop him? I thought this was officers only." I assured the lieutenant it was, but asked him, "Have you ever tried to disarm a seven-foot commie soldier carrying a machine pistol and two grenades?" We finally agreed to let it go—the commie was probably an officer anyway.

Except for details of recruiting and disposal of funds, we ran Reno Square for almost three months. It came to be known as "Pee Hei Loony's #5" after we discovered Mr. Loony controlled a chain of five houses in Tsingtao, including the famous "House of a Thousand Whores" and the "First Class Brothel"—at whose front door, marked with those words, dozens of Marines (including me) had their pictures taken without venturing indoors. Pee Hei Loony treated me like a #1 son. The fact that I would not accept money under the table only made me more beloved.

As for the Marine commandant and the Division Surgeon, I suppose their attitude toward our managing a whorehouse was the classic service approach: if it doesn't bite or shoot back, ignore it. We were never bothered as to procedure throughout the time, and we had the cleanest, venereally speaking, clients in Tsingtao, the lowest disease rate, at least.

But one day I was called again by another motherly j.g. who informed me that as of 1 December, Reno Square, or Pee Hei Loony's #5, would be open to the public, i.e., the enlisted men, and that a group of Navy corpsmen not attached to the Marines would take over pro station duties.

I broke the news to Pee Hei Loony, "Seek Preasure?," June Haver, Hedy and the rest in as Oriental a fashion as I knew how. There were sad cries of, "No, no, Joe," "boo how," "very bad" and vows to stab themselves from some of the girls, or it seemed thus to my loving, but untutored ear.

Anyway, we loaded our jeep and waved farewell. Back in the barracks, we never talked about our strange duty, even among ourselves. Accumulating points, one by one we corpsmen returned to the states. I was among the last. In the years since, I have not met or heard of the others. They fell, I trust, into suitable civilian occupations.

And though I never revisited Pee Hei Loony's #5, I still see the looming front entrance on the narrow, cobblestone street, still hear the birdlike twitter of the girls, see their doll-like faces and their wonderfully attractive, swaying way of walking. And it still breaks my heart to remember.

Chance Encounters
Presidents I have Known (Sort of)

Ronald Reagan
as host of TV's "Death Valley Days."

*Top, Philadelphia Naval Hospital brass awaiting the
Commander-in-Chief, Franklin D. Roosevelt.
Bottom, my one shot of the Chief as he whizzes by.*

Franklin D. Roosevelt

*I*n the Fall of 1944 I was a Navy Medical Corpsman stationed at Philadelphia Naval Hospital. The hospital was in south Philadelphia, not far from the big Philadelphia Naval Yard. I had been assigned to work in the photography lab, not because I was a photographer but because the high speed Mimeograph duplicating machine was there and I had been put in charge of the hospital's duplicating department. I didn't know as much about high speed duplication as I did photography. I had at least snapped pictures with my little Kodak Bullet camera (price one dollar) when I was a boy.

Uncle Sam never seemed to find the right place for me. I went to Great Lakes Naval Training Center and sang with the Bluejacket Choir, but wasn't quite good enough to gain permanent status. I worked in the post office branch for a while, but the Navy had too many professional mail handlers to keep me.

I eventually was made a Hospital Corpsman but because I could type I was never assigned to full time ward duty. As for the duplicating department assignment, I guess personnel figured since I could type I could cut the stencils which were used on the Mimeograph machine.

I had had a little newspaper experience as a civilian, and when the captain of the hospital decided to publish a station paper, my immediate superior in the photography department, a Danish native named

Lieutenant Gravessen, volunteered me for the job, so "Editor" was added to my duties. Gravessen, a professional photographer, was a decent guy so my job became, as was said in the Navy, "Good Duty." By being careful that a message from the captain was carried on Page 1 of each issue of the station paper, and by being sure no one satirized the captain, the medical staff or the U. S. Navy, I gained a certain amount of behind-the-scenes power.

Working with the Mimeograph machine and editing the station paper involved about three days a week. Therefore, being in the photo lab, I drifted into photography, starting in the darkroom developing and printing. Pretty soon I developed (no pun, please) into "a good hand" as the Navy liked to put it, with a camera. When it was announced that President and Commander-in-Chief Franklin D. Roosevelt was going to visit the Philadelphia Naval Yard and the Philadelphia Naval Hospital, our captain was aglow and ordered Gravessen to have every photographer on duty for the visit—and that included me.

Lieutenant Gravessen, knowing our captain fancied a rivalry with the much larger Naval Yard, ordered his two Photographers Mates (the official Navy rating) to go to the Yard and follow the President around there, possibly showing up the Yard's photographers with superior work. I would function as a back-up to the hospital's photo staff. One of the beliefs our captain held (shared by us Medical Corpsmen) was that the quality of the hospital personnel was much higher than that of the "swabbies" of the Naval Yard.

As happens so often in life, things didn't turn out the way they had been planned for the presidential visit. The morning of the visit it was announced, at the very last moment, that President Roosevelt would not stop at the hospital, but would merely drive by the front gate on Patterson Avenue. Our captain hurriedly ordered all the administrative officers and as many off duty nurses as could be on hand to muster at the front gate. Gravessen, unable to reach the Photographers Mates who were wandering around the Naval Yard, ordered me to grab up a shot bag and a camera and photograph the Commander-in-Chief—and be sure and also get a picture of the captain.

It was a cold, rainy day and (as we later learned) no day at all for the ailing President Roosevelt to be riding around in the presidential

Packard with the top down. The President had started late on his campaign for a fourth term, concerned as he was with the war, but Wendell Wilke of Indiana seemed to be making a strong appeal with his One World philosophy, so the old campaigner set out to campaign. We knew Franklin D. Roosevelt favored the Navy over other branches of the service, having been Assistant Secretary of the Navy, so in passing up the naval hospital, he may have figured he already had our vote.

As I reached the front gate, along with the official crowd, some Navy officer stopped me and said I couldn't do the photography: I wasn't a Photographers Mate. Typical Navy attitude—the right way, the wrong way and the Navy way—but you can't budge a bureaucrat, so I was about to try another exit when the captain himself called the bureaucrat over and apparently cleared me as an official Navy photographer. Since I was the only photographer in sight (the newspaper photographers were waiting for the President in downtown Philadelphia) I had gained the wartime status of "Imperative."

Several minutes before the President's car reached our street, Secret Service men came along setting up the rules, one of them even making the captain and his crew of brass step back away from the curb. (Could this have been a former enlisted man?)

"Are you an official Navy photographer?" another Secret Service man demanded of me. There were no brightly colored press tags available for this simple drive-by.

"Yes sir," I replied smartly, which was the way the Bluejacket's Manual said an enlisted man should reply to a superior officer.

"Let's see your credentials," the SS man demanded. I didn't have anything but my Navy ID card, which showed me officially as one of Uncle Sam's sailors.

"You can ask the captain," I said.

The SS man peered around and asked me, in rather scornful tones, "Yeah? Who's he?"

He looked over the crowd when I said simply, "Over there," not daring to raise a finger to point. To a Secret Service man assigned to guard the Commander-in-Chief, even a Navy captain (the equivalent of a bird colonel) lacked rank, but the SS man seemed to accept my defense.

"Okay," he said. "Where do you plan to shoot the President?"

Before I could stop I said, "I don't plan to shoot the President."

The SS man gave me a look of scorn and said, "Do you want to do this or not? If so, get serious. I'm not here to make jokes."

"Sorry, sir," I said, abashed, as, unquestionably, I should have been.

"Now, again, where do you plan to stand?"

"I thought I would climb that pedestal by the gate," I said. It made a wonderful camera site, a tall brick structure which would put me about four feet above the crowd.

"Nope. You can't be situated above the President and shoot down on him."

"Well," I mourned, "I guess I'll just stand here."

"You must not stand beyond this line," he said, then relented. "I guess it's all right if you lean over it a little. But stand there. Don't make any sudden gestures in the President's direction." He looked at my 4 x 5 Speed Graphic. "Are you going to use a flash bulb?"

He was no photographer, that's for sure. The day was half-dark by now and threatening to come down a frog-strangler, as West Texans liked to put it, so, of course, I was going to use a flash.

"Well, if you use a flash be sure the bulb is already in place, and let me see it."

"What if I need to get two pictures?"

"You will not wet a bulb and insert it in the flash gun," he said, "and if you are seen doing it you are subject to punishment."

I might point out for modern readers that most photographers, using a flash gun, always stuck their wet tongue to the end of the bulb to assure better electrical contact. Whether the idea was mythical or not, photographers did it without thinking.

"What kind of punishment?" I asked, not trying to be smart but from simple curiosity.

The Secret Service man looked at me narrowly, "You could get shot."

"What with?" I asked. I saw no shotguns or rifles anywhere.

"This," the SS man said, patting his overcoat. I detected a lust for power in his gesture. I gave in to him quickly.

As he watched, I loaded my Speed Graphic, letting him first glance over the slide cassette, then I licked and inserted the flash bulb.

"Okay now?"

"Okay," but grudgingly granted and from a great height.

I felt downright privileged as I stood there waiting for President Roosevelt to arrive. What other enlisted man had been grilled the way I'd been? I was sure the onlookers wondered about all the official talk and inspecting they had seen. Could this young sailor be kin to the President . . . or the Secret Service man, at least?

It was an impressive turnout of the brass, and I was pleased to be the only enlisted man to stand with that company. The six highest ranking hospital officials formed their separate line, standing at attention, Navy bridge coats properly buttoned, all wearing "scrambled eggs" on their cap brims. Behind them stood twenty nurses, not quite so much at attention, whispering among themselves. The nurses were all officers, of course, but it looked to me as if they had been selected for their looks; all were pleasing to the eye. They wore white nurses caps in their hair, white stockings and white shoes, and the beautiful long, high collared navy blue capes that set apart Navy nurses.

To the rear of the nurses was a conglomerate of mid-rank Navy officers, Marine officers and even an Army officer or two attached to the hospital. Civilians, some chattering in the cold, stood back along the curb for half a block in either direction.

Then, here came the cavalcade, the presidential Packard in front followed by two Cadillac limousines full of local and state bigwigs. President Franklin D. Roosevelt and two other men were riding in the rear seat of the Packard, the President on the right hand side nearest me. The top was down but the thick bulletproof windows were rolled up to form a protective shield against the cold as well as a potential assassin. Four Secret Service men rode with the President's car: two young, bareheaded men, each with a hand in an overcoat pocket, were at the rear corners, two older men, wearing felt hats, were riding the running boards at the car's front doors. I had to shoot quickly because one of the Cadillacs was coming up on my left, about to block the shot.

Just before I fired my flashbulb, President Roosevelt turned, seemed to look right at me, and smiled. He immediately turned face forward and rode past the saluting squad of officers without waving or acknowledging their salutes. Fala, the President's famous little Scottish terrier, if in the car, kept himself low in the seat, but when the Packard made an unscheduled stop a block away, I drew chuckles from some nurses when I suggested the halt was to let Fala use a fireplug.

My one-shot photo of the President came out well and I ran it three columns in the station newspaper—along with a two-column shot of the brass. The captain congratulated Lieutenant Gravessen on his staff's photo work. Not long after that I was shipped out attached to the U. S. Marines and did no more Naval photography. In April I was on my way to Guam with the Marines when President Roosevelt's death was announced.

A Brash Youth: A Presidential Story, But Not Mine

The late Jack Maguire was a friend who did a lot of the same things I had done: been a newspaper reporter, authored several Texas books, and written a weekly column about the Lone Star State. In addition to all that, he shared my intense love for railroads.

In 1936, when he was a junior in Denison (Texas) High School, Jack was dreaming of going to college but recognized that thanks to the Depression, it was a next to impossible dream. Jack's father was a Katy railroad fireman who had lost his regular run and whose work as an "extra" bought groceries, but little more.

But in April Jack won the twenty-five dollar first prize in an essay writing contest on fire prevention, and, as Jack said, "it rekindled my smoldering ambition to go to college." Winning so much money for a mere 965 words aroused another smoldering ambition—to be a journalist. Going to college and majoring in journalism would kill two birds with one stone, only, where was the stone coming from?

His twenty-five dollars would pay a semester's tuition in North Texas State College (now the University of North Texas), but the dorm fee, he found, was an added twenty-four dollars a month, and there would be incidentals. There was no assurance of help from the family purse.

Jack said, "Neither of my parents had gone beyond high school and

Jack Maguire was persuasive enough to stop the Chief. Shown here in his high school band uniform.

they saw no sound reason why their son needed to go to college, especially to study journalism. Just because I'd won an essay writing contest didn't prove to them I could write for a living."

Jack decided if he wanted to become a reporter he should try for a job at the local source, *The Denison Herald*. He'd never been inside a newspaper office, but he walked in, asked to see Mr. Shelby, the editor, and was ushered to his cubbyhole. Shelby looked like an editor from old Central Casting: horn-rim glasses, a trimmed mustache, sleeves rolled up with collar open. Jack showed him a copy of his prize-winning essay and told him he wanted to be a journalist and planned to go to college to study journalism if he could make some money. He asked for a summer job as a cub reporter. He would do it for five dollars a week.

The editor gave a cynical smile, "Son," he said, "I am hounded every day by experienced reporters who are willing to work ten hours a day, six days a week for twenty dollars a week. Why take on a cub even at five dollars a week?"

The implication that he wasn't even worth five dollars hurt Jack's sixteen-year-old pride. Knowing nothing about how the newspaper business worked, he nevertheless decided to gamble.

"Mr. Shelby," he said, "I'll make you a bet. If I can find a news story so big you'll run it on page one with an eight-column headline, will you give me a job?"

The editor stared over his glasses at Jack for a long time, then laughed. "I can't turn down a sure thing, so I'll take the bet. Get me a story like that and you'll get a job—but you can't win otherwise, son. Not even Franklin D. Roosevelt could convince me to hire an inexperienced cub."

Jack left the office dejected. The day's edition was coming off the press as he walked by the pressroom and he talked a pressman into giving him a copy. A story on page one jumped out at him: It was announced that in June President Franklin D. Roosevelt was coming to Texas to open the Texas Centennial Exposition in Dallas. Jack remembered the editor's remark that not even Franklin D. Roosevelt could cause him to hire a cub. Then, just as in the comic strips, a light came on in young Jack's head.

The President traveled by train in 1936, and Jack, having grown up in a railroad family, knew there were only two major rail routes between Dallas and Washington: one via Texarkana, the other at Denison. In those days of steam locomotives, all trains leaving Texas by way of Denison stopped there to change engine and crew. Jack wondered . . . was the President's train going to be routed through Denison?

Denison was headquarters for the Katy Railroad's general superintendent of transportation, the official who scheduled all train movements on the Katy line. His son and Jack were classmates, so Jack decided to call the superintendent at home. He asked him if he knew the President's travel plans in Texas. The official said he did: the White House had just confirmed the trip. The Presidential Special would enter Texas at Texarkana, but after the President opened the Centennial Exposition at Dallas, the special train would head north through Denison. Jack asked, would this Presidential Special make the usual engine and crew change here? Yes, the superintendent said, the Presidential Special would be stopping at 11 A.M. for the required changes, departing twenty minutes later.

That was all it took for Jack. That night he wrote President Roosevelt a letter. He explained his need for a summer job and told him of his bet with the newspaper editor. He pointed out that the President's train would be in Denison for twenty minutes, and although it was a small town, lots of people would like to see the President. If President Roosevelt would make a speech from the rear platform, he would be seen by hundreds of voters—and Jack would get a story and a job.

When Jack told the high school principal what he wanted to do, the principal was so proud of Jack's enterprise he allowed him to circulate the letter throughout school. More than 1,000 students signed it, along with Jack.

Within a short time, Jack received a reply from the White House: the President was pleased to accept his invitation. The news made the front page of *The Denison Herald* with the eight-column headline Jack had vowed he would create, and Jack became the town hero.

On June 13, 1936, POTUS (the code name for the train bearing the President of the United States), with Congressman Sam Rayburn and Texas Governor James V. Allred aboard—and Jack's father as fireman—pulled into the Denison Union Station where a crowd of 25,000 waited to greet President Roosevelt.

At the station, Jack presented Mrs. Roosevelt with a basket of flowers, President Roosevelt spoke from the rear platform for about ten minutes, and the train pulled out, heading back to Washington.

Editor Shelby didn't renege on their bet, Jack got the job at five dollars a week, but had to furnish his own typewriter. He used half of his twenty-five dollar essay prize check to buy a much-used L.C. Smith, which he treasured to the end of his career.

And there is a footnote. Months later, Eleanor Roosevelt, on a lecture tour, was to stop at Southeastern State University in Durant,

Oklahoma, twenty miles from Denison. She invited Jack to the lecture and to have lunch with her. During the meal she asked, "Jack, what have you ever done about that incident with Franklin?" Jack wasn't sure what she meant. He told her it had gotten him the job, and it looked like he was going to be able to go to college.

Mrs. Roosevelt said she understood that, but didn't Jack think it was rather unusual for a sixteen-year-old high school student to get the President of the United States to make a speech—just to help him win a bet? She said it was a story some national magazine might publish.

Jack, in his inexperience, hadn't thought of that, but he was bright enough to recognize a good tip. He followed Mrs. Roosevelt's suggestion and wrote a short piece titled, "The Happiest Moment of My Life." It was his first sale to a national magazine, but he hoped Mrs. Roosevelt never saw it in print. The magazine in which it appeared was *Modern Romance.*

A Presidential Concert

*M*uch prior to the time she and I made our unlooked for meeting after my trip to Maine *(See p.194 for this story)*, Judy had a chance encounter that involved unusual people and unusual results. Her father, John M. Dalton, a lawyer, was a friend of Harry S. Truman before that Missouri stalwart became President. John Dalton, having been an appointed officer of the Missouri Supreme Court during the Depression, was edging toward politics himself. (He later became Governor of Missouri.)

Judy and her family were living in the little town of Kennett, down in the "bootheel" of Missouri—where that state intrudes into northern Arkansas. That fall it was announced that President Harry Truman would make his first home state appearance since becoming president. A Legionnaire, he would attend an American Legion Fair in Caruthersville, Missouri, the old steamboat town on the Mississippi River, not many miles to the east of Kennett. John Dalton told the family he thought they should visit the President, but Judy's mother couldn't go, so father and daughter made the trip. John Hall Dalton, the older brother, was in the U. S. Navy.

Judy was an attractive little girl, the only child in the behind-the-scenes Truman party, and one of the entourage took over the job of entertaining her. President Truman was among his own Missouri people, and he made the most of it. David McCullough, in his classic biography, *Truman*, describes how the President "paused in his morning walk to spit in the Mississippi River—an old local rite, he explained to astonished reporters." McCullough adds: "He held open court in a drug store, went to the races, signed autographs on napkins and blank checks, posed with Legionnaires on a mock locomotive [and] rang the bell." *The Washington Post* said Truman did everything "except have himself shot from the mouth of a cannon."

Biographer McCullough also notes: "He [Truman] played the piano in the little hotel dining room." That needs some expansion, to wit: At the end of the public part of the affair, Judy, her father and the President and his party were in the hotel and President Truman

Harry S. Truman
and his daughter Margaret.

talked to Judy with the consideration and attention paid to a woman of voting age.

"Do you play a musical instrument?" he asked. Judy said that she took piano. "I'll bet you're good at it," President Truman said. Judy said she was only medium good as a piano player. The President went to the dining room upright piano and said to Judy, "Play us a piece, honey." Judy was too embarrassed and flustered to do it. She said she wouldn't dare play for President Truman.

"Well then," he said, "I'll play for you."

The President announced, "I'm dedicating this 'concert' to young Judy Dalton." While she sat on the piano bench with him, President Truman played his favorite, "The Missouri Waltz." The news photographers loved it. Not many young girls have been honored by a presidential serenade while the serenader was in the nation's highest office!

Lyndon Johnson's Long Memory

This story starts a good many years before it ends. In the summer of 1948, fresh out of college, I went to work for the *Abilene* (Texas) *Reporter-News.* I'd never seen Congressman Lyndon Baines Johnson, so I was delighted when the paper's political writer invited me to drive with him to Anson, the county seat of Jones, the next county. Johnson was to visit by way of helicopter. The use of a helicopter was a campaign first in Texas. If this were an ordinary campaign for senator, there wouldn't be any point in Lyndon Johnson flying around the state, appearing at little towns like Anson (population 2,700), in West Texas, which

Lyndon Baines Johnson

was not his political home turf. But running against Coke Stevenson, Johnson was going to need every scrap of vote he could get. Coke Stevenson had been a popular wartime governor of Texas, the portrait of "Old Mr. Texas": a tall, slender (very successful!) rancher, rugged with honesty; uprightness written all over his tanned, mature face— the stereotype of a Senator from the Great Southwest.

Congressman Johnson was seen by a lot of Texas Democrats as being "too Washington," too ambitious and too sly (this was when winning the Texas Democratic runoff was "tantamount to election"). He'd been Franklin Roosevelt's hand-picked boy—but Roosevelt was dead. Coke Stevenson had been drafted out of retirement to run against Johnson, and was conducting a strong campaign. Johnson's political life was on the line. He'd lost to W. Lee O'Daniel in the same Senate race in 1942 and if Stevenson defeated him now Johnson might (with luck) remain a congressman, but nothing more.

I was as much interested in the helicopter as I was the candidate; helicopters were a rare species of bird, having been introduced only toward the end of World War II. Johnson had staged a political coup by engaging a helicopter with which to campaign.

The political writer and I got to Anson ahead of time, parking on the edge of the vacant field where the helicopter was to come to earth. When it appeared, some thirty or so minutes late (politicians are always late) everyone was peering skyward, captured by the sight of this dragon-fly of the air that hovered, with a great whoosh, and was gently descending straight down.

Suddenly, a voice boomed out, the voice of God, speaking from heaven, catching us off guard: "My fellow Texans . . . this is your next senator, Lyndon Johnson." Then, when the helicopter was about ten feet off the ground, a door suddenly opened from which a white, ten-gallon hat came flying along with another booming announcement: "My hat is in the ring!"

The instant the helicopter touched the ground, Lyndon Johnson leaped out, retrieved his hat, jammed it on his head and began pressing the flesh (as he liked to call it). He moved quickly, looking into the eyes of each person as he shook his or her hand. The political writer told me, afterward, that the first hand Johnson had grabbed was that of the Jones County Republican chairman, and LBJ was in such a hurry the County Democratic chairman and the Anson mayor (Democrat) couldn't catch up with him. I was amused to see the candidate pressing the flesh of a Mexican-American cotton picker who had come running from a nearby patch and was grinning delightedly, chattering away in machine gun Spanish. He was reluctant to let go of Johnson's hand, following the candidate along, but I caught the phrase *"el presidente!"* a couple of times, so that helped.

With a waving, embracing gesture to the crowd, the candidate climbed back in the helicopter (that had never cut its engines) and it rose majestically into the blue. The crowd, which had stood startled and stunned when he was among them, suddenly gave a cheer toward the disappearing bird: LBJ all the way!

Lyndon Johnson won the election by only eighty-seven votes, after a recount, and those eighty-seven were bitterly contested from Texas to the Supreme Court. But voter lists and election boxes mysteriously disappeared and the Supreme Court ruled it had no jurisdiction over the state election. It was the tightest U. S. Senate race in American history. And it took nearly two decades for Lyndon Johnson to outlive the sneering nickname, "Landslide Lyndon."

★ ★ ★

By 1954 I faced problems that took my mind off Lyndon Johnson and politics. I had bought a small house in Abilene, under the Veterans Housing bill, my sole source of income being the sagging business of the retail bookstore I owned and managed. In addition, my wife and I had a young child, so we had lots of problems, though only one was major: larger outgo than income. But through it all, tough and tougher, I bragged to my wife, we never missed a house payment.

My plans for the book business had proved to be too grandiose. At the time I bought the book store I had been a reasonably popular newspaper columnist, so I thought it good advertising to write a weekly book column. I quickly discovered it was one thing to be paid to write a column and quite another to pay to have one printed. I soon had to abandon weekly newspaper advertising.

Then the local television station came to me with a proposition. I could have a weekly TV spot at very low rates if I could accept a certain shirt-tail quality to the time: whatever time was left after the

10 P.M. news—hours between the news and midnight, when the station went off the air, were usually bare of revenue. My twenty cents-on-the-dollar rate was better for the station than nothing at all. Some weeks I could end up with as much as fifteen minutes of TV air time for less than the cost of that weekly newspaper column.

I won't belabor the program itself except to say, it was pioneer television. My two-year-old son Geoffrey whimpered in terror the first time he saw my face on television. He thought they had shoved me into that little box and wouldn't let me out.

I think we performed a television first, if not in the Union, certainly in Texas: We broadcast a genuine wedding which we staged (with a single camera) right there in the station's big studio for live presentations. My associate, Mary Katherine McDougall, not only came up with the idea but came up with the bride and groom, a big wedding cake, and all kinds of gifts for the newlyweds (I presented them with a family Bible).

But that night when I returned home, I found my wife in tears. A Western Union delivery boy had arrived about 9 P.M. with a collect telegram from the mortgage company in Fort Worth which held the mortgage on our little home. My wife refused to pay. The delivery boy told her to go ahead and open it; the sender would have to pay anyway. The telegram was brusque without an ameliorating clause: if you don't start making timely house payments we'll cut your head off—or words to that effect.

I was outraged. The payment deadline for the monthly payment (a huge seventy-nine dollars per month) was the fifteenth. I had cut it very close sometimes, but had never missed a payment and only a delay of the U. S. mail had caused any payment to be late. Despite the time of night (it was approaching the witching hour) I drove downtown to the Western Union office and dispatched two night letters of protest, asking if this was any way to treat an ex-GI who had risked his life in the service of Uncle Sam, who was upright and honest in the community, who, with a young wife and family, was trying to fulfill the American Dream the hard way, running his own small business, never missed a payment, etc. etc. (Night Letters gave you space to vent your spleen and tell your virtues without having to hock your billfold.) I sent one Night Letter to Congressman Omar Burleson, who represented our part of West Texas in the House, and whom I had interviewed several times during my journalistic days. The other went to Senator Lyndon Baines Johnson, whom I had never met, and who had not been near West Texas since the 1948 helicopter tour.

Next morning when I opened my bookstore at 8:30 A.M., Central Standard Time, sticking in the door handle was a reply from Senator Johnson's staff. The Senator was out of Washington but would be notified of my telegram the minute he walked back in his office. Meanwhile a query would be made to the Fort Worth mortgage company and further more a copy of my telegram was being sent to the Veterans Administration.

Within a week I had received copies of the correspondence between Senator Johnson's office and the mortgage company, which came close to denying it had sent the threatening telegram, saying I had misinterpreted it, and claiming all sorts of evil credit practices on my part.

Well, I must say the carbons began flowing in to me: between Johnson and the mortgage company, between the Veterans Administration and Johnson, then between the VA and the mortgage company. The VA got tougher and tougher on the Fort Worth people, and I gloried in it. Eventually the mortgage company promised there would be no more late-night telegrams such as I had received, and the company would be more careful in harassing veterans, making sure the offenders had truly violated the contract. It was a complete victory and I received carbons at every stage of the mortgage company's defeat. Senator Johnson was chairman of some powerful committee that controlled much of the Veterans Administration's operation. That surely helped. I never received a reply from Omar Burleson, my Congressman. Sometime later I asked him if he got my telegram and he said, yes, but what had I expected him to do about it? I told him to forget it, the problem had been taken care of.

Several years later, when I was Editorial Page Editor of the late *Dallas Times Herald*, Vice President Lyndon Baines Johnson called on the paper in a surprise visit and, both the publisher and the company president being out of town, some of the news staff were allowed to sit around the Directors Table and talk with the Vice President. He proved to be a most effective face-to-face politician. Even if you disagreed with him you could not help believing his earnest answers.

After we had spent half an hour with him, LBJ insisting that the head of the Printers' Union be brought up for a visit, the Vice President made a quick tour of the building. But before he started I approached him, apologizing for holding him up and told him I had a long-standing debt of gratitude I owed him, although I was sure it was so minor he had forgotten it. He asked me for the details, and I related how the Fort Worth mortgage company had sent me the threatening telegram and how his office had done such a fine job of taking care of it—and he stopped me.

"What th' hell do you mean I've forgotten it? And it was me that did it, not my office. Hell yes, I remember. Gave me a chance to kick th' butt of (and he mentioned a well known Texas financier who controlled several mortgage companies). That s.o.b. never supported me with a single dime in a single race. Damn right, I remember," he shook my hand and grinned, "Always proud to meet a fellow Texan." My kind of President!

Having a Drink With an Actor

*I*n the late years of the 1950s, I held the lofty title of Amusements Editor of the *Abilene Reporter-News*. I wanted to call it Arts Editor, but the publisher thought "Arts" sounded effete, and God knows, I didn't want to sound effete.

My duties included writing afternoon features, reviewing movies, covering music concerts, art shows—with the help of my friend, Professor Norman Whitefield, head of the Abilene Christian Art Department. Theatrical productions were a major concern since Abilene had a very active community theater, two colleges and a university, all with strong drama departments, as well as a large, energetic high school and Dyess Air Base, with many thespians, dancers, musicians and other performers. I was also in charge—unofficially—of taking care of all sorts of artists and performers who happened to be in town.

One afternoon I got a call from a wealthy, and very likeable oilman named French Robertson. "A. C.," French said, "you're the movie critic or whatever you call it, aren't you?" I agreed. "Well, we've got a guy coming to spend the night with us—the one and only Ronald Reagan. My favorite movie actor. You like him?"

I said I had liked him a lot in *King's Row* and *Voice of the Turtle*. Very versatile actor.

"Well, why don't you come by and have a drink with us when you get off? I'm gonna pick him up at the airport, let him take a nap, and we'll have drinks 'bout five-thirty or so. You're a martini man, aren't you?" Martinis were drink-of-choice for all would-be intellectuals. I agreed to his proposals.

Ronald Reagan was in Abilene to make a speech to either the Abilene Chamber of Commerce or the West Texas Chamber of Commerce. He was making speeches all over the west for General Electric which sponsored his television show. When the appointed time rolled around I drove out to French's house, a fine structure designed and decorated by the best professionals in Texas. When French came to the door, Ronald Reagan was with him and the three of us quickly made friends. French had a beautiful young daughter named Miranda and it helped loosen up the actor when she dropped in to meet him and flattered him unmercifully. I knew Miranda quite well because she was part of the Abilene Community Theater group. (That was also how French knew I was a martini man—from me, as critic, attending parties his daughter had given for the theater crowd.)

After my first martini (French declared he and Reagan were one up on me) we got into a serious conversation about films and film making. French, like every wealthy Texas oilman of that period had been approached to bankroll a film or two—one offering a "big" part to Miranda if her daddy came in. Reagan not only advised against that kind of investment but warned that the road was hard, even if daddy did put two or three million in the production. This was a day when a six-million dollar picture was about average.

From films and filmmaking we drifted (my second martini) into political talk, and Reagan was quite open in his likes and dislikes, and not very conservative, as I recollect our talk. He admitted the field of politics attracted him and he said one reason General Electric was having him make these speeches was that the corporation felt he had a way of lecturing on American public values without sounding like he was "talkin' politics." I will admit, I was quite impressed, but thought of nothing political for him—who ever heard of a Hollywood movie actor getting into politics above the precinct level?

When I was leaving, Ronald Reagan stood between French and me, putting his arms around us (he was taller than either of us), and declared, "Boys . . . we're the best kind of Americans. We're self-made men." French and I nodded agreement. "I know ol' French here is," Reagan said, squeezing the oilman. French said, "Boy, all you got to do is read a few of my old bank statements to see that I came up th' hard way."

"I know damn well I am," Reagan said, then squeezing my shoulder added, "and I'll bet ol' A. C. is too, aren't you?" He looked at me smiling, I hope with pride.

"I'm one of the originals," I said, thinking of my $400 a month salary. "I'm still fightin' th' good fight!"

With another squeeze, Reagan laughed loudly and said again, "Self-made men, by God. The best kind of American there is." As I left them, he and French were still congratulating each other (and me *in absentia*, I trust) for being self-made men. I never met Ronald Reagan again.

Why George Bush (The First) Owes Me a Case of Beer

I spent several years in the 1960s as Editor of the Editorial Page at the old *Dallas Times Herald*, an afternoon newspaper which, alas, in 1991 went the way of too many afternoon newspapers. However, in the 1960s the *Times Herald* was a powerful force in Dallas and while it was not exactly a liberal organ, it did allow my staff and me some latitude on the editorial page. I hadn't rushed into the job naively. I knew that often the political candidate choices of management were not going always to be mine, so when I was offered the post, I said I would not write national and state political endorsement editorials. This stipulation was granted and somebody from the executive chambers downstairs wrote them. (I might add this information: the political stance of a newspaper is determined by the publisher, not the editors or writers.)

But this isn't a discussion of newspaper politics. As Editorial Page Editor I met numbers of interesting or important-for-the-moment individuals. I was never surprised at how many people (beyond politicians) wanted us to make note of their existence. You have heard the old media plea: say anything about me you please, but spell my name right.

The Executive Editor of the *Times Herald* during my time was a veteran Texas newsman named Felix R. McKnight, and although he and I maintained a continuing editorial war—he killed plenty of my columns and editorials—it was not a petty or spiteful relationship. I liked Felix. One afternoon in 1964 he called me down to the paper's lobby saying he wanted me to meet the Republican candidate for the U. S. Senate, George Herbert Walker Bush of Houston. I joined the two men in the lobby and I told George Herbert Walker Bush I had kept up with him, as an oil man, because we were both West Texans. He had lived for several years in Midland and I was from Abilene. We had an amiable meeting, Felix hinting from time to time that I might write a column pointing out what a nice man Bush was in person, and how well he understood Texas business—which at that time was spelled o-i-l.

Ultimately that conversation in the *Times Herald* lobby got around to Vietnam. From having initially supported President Kennedy's use of American armed forces in that nation, I was beginning to question it: why were we not only staying but increasing our presence? However, I knew the official *Times Herald* stand might not match mine, so I wrote about Vietnam gingerly, and to be fair to management, I don't think anyone downstairs knew what to think about the conflict.

George Bush, though a Republican, supported the announced American efforts and when I suggested that we were getting into some sticky situations, such as the predicted defoliation of the Ho-Chi Minh Trail in Laos and Cambodia, he disagreed. "I don't think we (the U. S.) will do that," he said stoutly, "it's not necessary." I believed it might happen within a few weeks. We gave the back-and-forths of our arguments, in friendly fashion, and at some point George Bush said he'd bet me a bottle of beer my timetable was off. I said I would take the bet. Felix McKnight said, "Let's not quibble over a *bottle* of beer. Make it a *case* of beer." Bush and I again agreed and I threw in, "A case of *good* beer," which was accepted.

Well, the U. S. did start its defoliation war well inside the time limit I had set. George Bush lost his senate race but next election won a seat in Congress from the Houston district. Within a very few years he had become a national power in the Republican Party. He was Ambassador to the United Nations, then Chief Liaison Officer for the U. S. office in Bejing and later was the very upright head of the C.I.A. And, of course, became Chief Executive of the United States in 1988 after serving as Vice-President under President Ronald Reagan.

Sometime in the 1980s he and I shared teaser lines on the cover of *American West* magazine, wherein he wrote about coming to West Texas and getting in the oil business and I wrote about my West Texas frontier granny. But despite hints in high places, I had not gotten my case of (good) beer when, in 1988, the case became moot. After my heart transplant that year I was forbidden alcohol, even beer. Only non-alcohol beverage, good non-alcohol beverage, was allowed.

★ ★ ★

The next time I saw President George H. W. Bush again in person was in 1998, thirty-four years after our case-of-beer bet. We were at a huge "Writers Breakfast" at the Texas Governor's Mansion in Austin, part of the annual Texas Book Festival literary conference which was sponsored by his daughter-in-law, Laura Bush. I was feeling a warm glow because Laura Bush, the beautiful Texas First Lady, had given me a big hug when she greeted me at the front door. She and I had met a couple of years before and, having been a librarian, she was familiar with my books.

That first time we met she had taken Judy and me on a private tour of the Mansion after discovering I had never before been in the house that Sam Houston haunts. Judy was particularly interested in the restoration because her father, John M. Dalton, had been Governor of Missouri when her mother, Jerrie, helped initiate the beautiful restoration of the Show-Me state's Governor's mansion.

At the "Writers Breakfast," President Bush and I shook hands and I mentioned I had met him years before and he remembered Felix McKnight, but I could tell he didn't remember me. Later that morning

A. C. Greene receiving the "Texas Bookend Award" from then, Texas First Lady Laura Bush.

I received the first annual Texas Book Festival's "Book End Award," and Laura Bush made the formal presentation. The award itself, made of Texas limestone, is so heavy it took both hands for the First Lady to present it to me. Later, when George Bush tried to talk about the new book he and Brent Scowcroft had written, unruly (and pointless) hecklers disrupted his speech until they had to be taken from the Legislative Chamber of the capitol, where the event took place.

★ ★ ★

George H. W. Bush, in an indirect way, also caused me to miss having breakfast with Walter Cronkite and his wife. In 1991, Judy and I were in West Rockport, Maine, visiting with Fred and Jerrie Smith (where Fred, in 1989 had asked if I intended "taking yourself out among the ladies again.")

On the first day Judy and I got to West Rockport in 1991, Fred reported he had gotten a call from their yacht that Steve Ross and his wife, Courtney, were coming for dinner. I had chanced to meet Steve Ross in 1984 at a Camden waterfront fish house while visiting Fred and Jerrie. Steve and I had told "Old Navy" stories as we were both enlisted sailors in World War II. Courtney Sale, the Texas girl he later married, was with him and I had known her in Dallas. We all had so much fun Steve offered to fly my wife Betty and me back to Texas if we would stay over for a day, but I thought it would be inconvenient, bringing a plane up from New York. I didn't realize he had a Gulf Stream and two pilots waiting at Owl Head, a few miles from Camden.

So, that 1991 night after one of Jerrie Smith's great dinners, Steve, now CEO of Time-Warner, entertained with card tricks and sleight-of-hand (he was of near pro status). As he and Courtney departed that night, he said we were all to meet early the next morning at his yacht, "Liberty," berthed in Camden, he had a surprise for us. It turned out the surprise was to be breakfast with the Cronkites aboard their yacht, also in Camden harbor. However, during the night President George Bush had called the Cronkites asking them to come visit him and Barbara in Kennebunkport, so, with great apologies to the Rosses, they pulled out early for the sail down to Kennebunkport— thus no chance to encounter with the Cronkites for Judy and me. Steve Ross died a few months after that. He had the reputation of being a ruthless business competitor, but I found him generous, considerate and thoughtful. Maybe it was because we were the last WWII enlisted sailors who had not promoted themselves to officer rank.

★ ★ ★

There is yet another chapter to the Bush stories, a joyful chapter that was almost swept away by the disastrous tragedies of forty-five hours later.

Laura Bush, already showing herself to be one of the two or three most outstanding American First Ladies since Edith Bolling Wilson, had quickly become an active figure in national intellectual leadership within six months of her husband's inauguration as U. S. President in January 2001. Her face began to grace the covers of many magazines, and such newspapers as the *Washington Post* carried articles by her on libraries, schoolteachers, and books. Texas-born (Midland) and trained (Southern Methodist University and the University of Texas at Austin) Laura Bush is careful to keep her own writings non-political; she just wants to encourage reading and the teaching of reading.

To this end, she, with the cooperation of the Library of Congress, founded the National Book Festival in Washington, D.C. The first annual festival was held September 7 and 8, 2001, free for the public. It is based on the successful Texas Book Festival, which she had begun in 1996 in Austin while she was First Lady of Texas. The first National Book Festival was a huge and inspiring success. Pavilions set on the lawn at the Library of Congress, with authors' readings, panels and exhibits from the Library, were soon full, with long lines awaiting entry. On Sunday, September 9, Mrs. Bush hosted a brunch in the White House for a number of Texas writers and others who had supported the Texas Book Festival. Although the invitation was addressed to Mr. and Mrs. A. C. Greene, Judy was already committed to a visit in Oregon where a sick friend of ours lived. My daughter Meredith took her place, at Judy's suggestion.

At the White House we were met by Jim Lehrer, the veteran Public Broadcasting System's news editor, an old friend from Dallas, who guided us to the brunch food room, and while I sat waiting for Meredith to return with a plate for me, someone slipped her arms around my shoulders, and I was astounded, and mightily pleased that it was First Lady Laura Bush. She told me she wanted to thank me for letting her quote from a couple of my articles about a library being my babysitter. Later, as she and I stood while numbers of people were taking pictures—of her, but they had to include me—I remarked that some were shooting my "bad side." Laura Bush laughed, "Well, let me get on the other side so you can have your 'good side' pictured." I could scarcely believe we were in the White House with America's First Lady.

President Bush was present and when we had arrived a long line was waiting to shake his hand. After the picture taking with the First Lady, Jim Lehrer came with a wheel chair borrowed from Liz Carpenter manned by a handsomely uniformed Naval White House attaché. As the young Naval officer pushed me I remarked to him that, as a Second Mate in World War II, he certainly outranked me. He smiled and said, "But look who's pushing the wheel chair!"

We approached President Bush, the line now down to four or five, and Jim Lehrer said, "President Bush, here's A. C. Greene." I stood from the wheel chair and the President said, "I've been wanting to meet you, Mr. Greene." There was a woman standing by him, apparently a friend or a White House staffer, and President Bush said to her, "This is A. C. Greene, one of our great writers." I smiled, demurring, "Mr. President, that's spreading it on a little thick."

President Bush said, "You think so? Well, in that case, I'll make it a decree!" Thus, I may be the only living writer who became great by Presidential Decree.

★ ★ ★

At the brunch there were many fellow Texas writers and, again, the guest list was non-partisan. President and Mrs. Bush were so gracious and popular the brunch became a good 'ol Texas reunion, without a hint of politics.

But today September 9, 2001, seems in another age, the calendar being ripped apart and hurled away two days later by the ghastly events that began on September 11, 2001.

A.C. standing between President George Bush and his daughter Meredith at the Sunday Brunch at the White House celebrating the First National Book Festival.

Chance Encounters
in the 1950s

Mickey Mantle

T. S. Eliot

He Went a Long Way From St. Louis

The first time I heard Thomas Stearns Eliot's poetry read aloud was during a brief period in 1942 when I attended the former Phillips University in Enid, Oklahoma. To help earn my tuition I had a job as night watchman on the Phillips campus. I was headquartered in the basement of the girls' dormitory, where one of my tasks was to make certain the water gauge of the big old Kewanee boiler located there was kept at a safe level. A stout steel door stood guard over the virtue of the young ladies overhead. Nothing protected me from the virtuous young ladies, however, and one cold February night, as I stepped on the porch of this dormitory to punch the time clock, a tub of freezing water (accompanied by gales of laughter) descended on my hunched-over shoulders. My whistling as I made my rounds, the young ladies reported, kept them awake.

At the time I lived there, Enid was its own world, sitting off to itself, on the map, and holding itself to be a little above other Oklahoma towns. It boasted an enormous annual wheat crop, two major oil companies headquartered there, and in those days before national television, a famous semi-pro basketball team, the Eason Oilers, made it a jewel in the sports crown. Enid's First Families had gained their acreage in the celebrated Cherokee Strip land rush of 1889. Three former residents had gone on to great contemporary fame: Marquis James, the Pulitzer Prize winning author, Sherman Billingsley, operator of The Stork Club and darling of New York's "cafe society" at the time, and Steve Owen, coach of the New York Giants pro football team.

My family rented a house on East Oklahoma, one of Enid's oldest streets. Marquis James was said to have lived in our house and the others lived nearby. That house had three assets which intrigued our family: a big basement (rare in Texas), a pull-down Murphy bed, and a brown-and-white mouse that appeared each evening and sat on its hindquarters, as though some former inhabitant had trained it thusly.

It is sufficient to say, with a job by night and classes by day I had little time for anything but studying and driving to and from work. Luckily, the secondhand Oldsmobile Eight my father owned—bought "almost new" with the odometer rolled back to only 38,000 miles— had a radio in it (a luxury automotive accessory then) and I used to tune in to the Oklahoma University radio station on my way to the Phillips campus. One night I heard three OU professors reading from and discussing two poems by T. S. Eliot: "Journey of the Magi" and "Sweeney among the Nightingales." It was the most powerful poetry I had heard. I was familiar with Eliot's name but somehow had missed the modern poetry courses where I might have encountered him. I sat in the car, listening, until the program was over, causing me to be late starting my watchman's job.

That night, as I made my rounds, I didn't whistle but tried to bring back some of the lines that had impressed me:

> *A cold coming we had of it,*
> *Just the worst time of year for a journey.*
>
> *And an old white horse galloped away in the meadow . . .*
>
> *Apeneck Sweeney spreads his knees /*
> *Letting his arms hang down to laugh . . .*
>
> *Bananas, figs and hothouse grapes . . . .*

★ ★ ★

A year later, in World War II service, I wanted to find a book of Eliot's poems but never seemed to have time to inquire until I was with the U. S. Marines at Camp Lejeune, North Carolina. At the

Hadnot Point library I found several of Eliot's poems in that great little collection, *The Oxford Book of Modern Verse* (1936 edition), now long outdated but with a priceless introductory essay by William Butler Yeats. I checked the book out three times, then discovered I was soon to be going overseas. I was alarmed. How could I give the book up until I'd at least *memorized* the Eliot poems—and I was (am) a slow memorizer.

James Graham Gray, a fellow Navy Corpsman (and a Williams College man), made the common sense suggestion that I steal the book and take it with us. He was an Eliot fan and he and I were going on the same overseas draft. I did not have to steal the book. Merriam Rothenberg, the librarian at Hadnot Point library said just report I had lost it and pay for a replacement. Which I did, and still have the receipt (for $2.17) signed by her and clipped in the battered copy of *The Oxford Book of Modern Verse* that I carried in my seabag during the year I spent in the Pacific and China with the 15th Marines.

A war correspondent from Milwaukee sat in my tent on Guam one night, a good bit of our beer ration consumed, and, by light of a Coleman lantern, read Eliot aloud from my book, getting wobblier and wobblier as he stumbled across "Rat's coat, crowskin, crossed staves . . . supplication of a dead man's hand . . . This broken jaw of our lost kingdoms . . . ." Putting down the book after reading the lines, "As the perpetual star / Multifoliate rose," he exclaimed, "What th' hell is a multifoliate rose?"

★ ★ ★

I was discharged from the U. S. Navy/Marines in April, 1946, and soared on the Burlington-Rock Island Railroad's luxurious Sam Houston Zephyr from Houston to my parents' home in Dallas. The first thing I did next morning (still in my Marine Corps uniform) was to go to Liz Ann McMurray's famous Dallas bookstore and ask if the store had *Collected Poems of T. S. Eliot*.

"Of course," the salesman said, "even in wartime we have never had fewer than five copies on hand." He brought me the yellow-jacketed book, I paid him the two dollars and fifty cents it was marked, and went into spasms of joy as I read the poems of T. S. Eliot on the trolley car headed toward Urbandale, the suburb where my parents lived. The ride and the reading combined joys, because streetcars and railroads ranked then and now only after poetry and music in my cultural Garden of Eden. Fifteen years later the man who sold the Eliot book to me, the late Everett DeGolyer, Jr., became a good friend, our friendship based as much on railroads as on poetry. His unparalleled collection of railroadiana became, along with his father's rare books, the starting point for the magnificent DeGolyer Library at Southern Methodist University. When we met again, Ev remembered me after all those years. "I was not accustomed to having uniformed U. S. Marines come seeking the poetry of T. S. Eliot," he said, in his unmistakable "Ev DeGolyer" drawl.

In my last years of college, service in the Navy having broken my higher education into two parts, I became something of a bore about Eliot. One girl I dated became almost as "converted" to Thomas Stearns as I was. When she married I accused her of carrying a copy of *Collected Poems* instead of a white Bible.

Later, when I was in the retail book business, I, too, never carried fewer than five copies of Eliot's collected poems. I was asked by the local newspaper to do an essay on the book that influenced me most. I did it on T. S. Eliot's poetry, and tried to express that feeling of alienation but inspiration I drew from his work. By then I had found *Four Quartets* and their beautiful messages. (But I mustn't become an Eliot evangelist; even I accept William Butler Yeats as perhaps a greater poet.)

Working for me in my bookstore had been a young woman named Nancy McMeans who was not only above average in brains and looks but had a quality of responsibility that was quickly recognized by anyone in charge of anything with which she was connected (the only girl-child, she had raised a bunch of brothers). After her time at my bookstore, when she attended the University of Texas at Austin, she became righthand woman for Harry Ransom, the famed Chancellor of the University for whom the University Humanities Research Center was later named.

I had been out of the book business by a few years when Nancy called me one day in the spring of 1958 and told me the University was bringing T. S. Eliot to Austin during his tour of the United States. Would I like to meet him? The only question was: when? Nancy did some behind the scenes arrangements so that after I got up at 2 A.M. and drove my wonderful 1952 Packard "400" down to the University, she was waiting to guide me to one of the sacred parking spots around the Administration Tower.

T. S. Eliot was with his new young wife Valerie and his American publisher, Robert Giroux, of Farrar, Straus and Giroux. Eliot, while a Nobel Prize winner, recognized the commercial side of literature, working as an editor and director for Faber and Faber, Ltd., a major British publisher. Once the U. T.'s "Eliot Day" program began, I had the best of both worlds. Nancy had not told anyone of her schemes involving her old boss, so the literature department of the University thought I was with Eliot's group, and the Eliot party presumed I was with the University. I think I carried off both roles successfully.

Some of the professors may have been more knowledgeable, having done dissertations on, or involving, Eliot's work, but I had an advantage; I read him with love. At one roundtable meeting I recalled a story that students at St. Louis University had sent Eliot a recording of the popular song, "You've Come a Long Way From St. Louis" (his birthplace), and he thanked them, noting, however, the final line: "But, baby, you've still got a long way to go." I asked if he still had the recording. Eliot broke into a grin (his smile was generally sweet but mild) and turned to Valerie. "We still have the record and play it often, don't we dear?" This little human touch seemed to delight him and he sometimes had me sit either by himself or his wife. (His blue wool sweater had a ravel at the "v" which added another humane touch.) He and Valerie were very much in love and she, who knew his poetry as much as anyone there, performed well as wife of a Nobel Prize poet.

At lunch the University had laid out a fine meal in the beautiful Wrenn Library and we ate with silverware made by Paul Revere himself. At one point Mr. Eliot asked us about Texas history in relation to the broader national scene. I seemed to have been the only one there who knew much Texas history. Although a British resident since 1914, Eliot was remarkably well versed in American affairs. But I mustn't make it sound as though I took over the day of T. S. Eliot. I wish I could have—but I didn't, by any means. However, as the afternoon was closing in and it was announced that the Eliots and Robert

Giroux must leave, I got up the nerve to ask the poet if he would autograph my copy of his *Collected Poems*, apologizing that it might be inconvenient, but he said, in his wonderful British accent, "Oh, not at all." Putting his arm around my shoulder, he walked with me to the tall south windows of the library—almost cathedral height—and he took out his pen and wrote in my book, "Inscribed for A. C. Greene, Esq. by T. S. Eliot." (I may have it buried with me.) When we turned back to the others, gathered in a crescent, they applauded—not for me but as a farewell to T. S. Eliot.

Driving back from Austin to Abilene, after that Eliot-filled day at the University of Texas, I stopped along the highway and wrote myself a note: if Betty, with child, produced a son, couldn't we name him Eliot? This she did a few months later, and Eliot became his name. In late 1962, after I had moved to Dallas and become Book Editor of the *Dallas Times Herald*, I wrote a column about T. S. Eliot, his poetry and its effect on me, and sent a clipping to him in London, enclosing a letter explaining that I had named a son for him after our meeting. He wrote back, in January, 1963, with a letter that concluded: "am honored, of course, by your naming your son Eliot and hope that he will find the name auspicious."

This letter, framed, is held so precious by that son, Eliot, and that father, me, that ownership of the document has been a continuing bone of contention between them, the father pointing out that the letter is addressed to him, the son asserting that since he is the subject of the letter, ownership naturally devolves on him.

Gabriel Blows at Midnight

Abilene, where I labored in the journalistic vineyard as overworked Amusements Editor, had not only been bone dry since 1902, but had (and has) three church related universities within its municipal boundaries—proper places with generally proper students. Hardin-Simmons University, the oldest (1891) and Southern Baptist, is located on the north side of the two-sided town (North Side and South Side). Abilene Christian University (1906) is affiliated with the

Church of Christ and is now the largest of the three schools. Its campus is at the northeast corner of the city. McMurry University (1923) is in the southern half of the city and is a United Methodist institution. I stipulate these dimensions and religious affiliations because they played a part in the style of entertainment each school imported as well as my ability to cover two events on the same night, none of the schools being within galloping distance of one another.

All three universities got as high quality musical performers as they could fiscally afford. As for theater productions, all the universities, as well as Abilene High School and Dyess Air Force Base, had unusually strong dramatics departments with outstanding directors, so one could always stir up a lot of good theatrical talk even if it wasn't always on stage.

But let me assure you, my job demanded quite a bit of walking the razor's edge, avoiding some of the denominational or religious factions that had a good deal of clout. There was no telling how your write-up might be interpreted. One time I casually mentioned in a write-up that researchers speculated Noah had beer aboard the ark. You would have thought I had announced the opening of a do-it-yourself brothel. I escaped by pointing out that the word beer didn't automatically imply alcoholic content—take "root beer," for example, but that didn't convince the true believers.

McMurry University more often than either ACU or H-SU had popular musicians on campus. One year the Four Freshmen visited and got a powerfully good reception. After my review of their show had been phoned in I went backstage and met the men. They were elated at the spontaneous nature of the applause. They had attended a small midwestern college, as I recall, starting their group as genuine freshmen. They felt at home at a school like McMurry. We went out for a bite and ended up at a late-night diner called The Dixie Pig and, again, they felt right at home in this sort of establishment.

The Four Freshmen, unlike some later musical successes, were genuine musicians; not only good vocalists but fine instrumentalists of strum, thump and toot varieties, often using unusual instrumentation for unusual harmonic effects.

We left The Dixie Pig and went back to the Hotel Wooten where they were staying up high on the fourteenth floor, or what was probably the thirteenth, but, of course, was not numbered that way. At least twice in its career, the big neon sign atop the Hotel Wooten shorted out and proclaimed, for all Abilene to ponder, "Hot - - Woo - - -." At any rate, we were gathered in a suite they had rented—ah, to think you could get a nice suite in a good hotel for twenty dollars a night— and were discussing music when I innocently asked what was the difference between a trumpet, a cornet and a flügelhorn. Two of them started to explain when Ken Albers, who seemed to be the leader, said why not get the three instruments and show me. When the men came back with the instruments, it was pointed out that the three were similar, in that they had cylindrical metal tubes, valves, and flared bells, but had differing ranges and tones. Each offered a slightly different "voice."

"Here, I'll show you," one of the instrumentalists said, taking up the coronet. He blew a few notes, then reached for the trumpet when Albers again interrupted.

"Hey . . . wait a minute. It's past midnight. Blow that thing inside here and you'll wake up the hotel."

It was decided that it might be better if we opened a window (that was in the days when you could open a hotel window) and let the sound slip away outdoors. No, no, we were not even slightly tipsy . . . remember, Abilene was bone dry; and so were we.

Through the open window there was a blast of the trumpet, notes from one of the special arrangements of The Four Freshmen. Then an additional dozen or so notes were squeezed from the coronet (squeezy-sounding compared to the trumpet), and finally a solo on the flügelhorn, rounder and fuller than the other two.

The results were unlooked for. Abilene still had a number of residences near the downtown—certainly near enough to the downtown to be clearly reached by such brazen calls from on high. Lights began popping on in a circle south and west. A good religious town, several of the more devout citizens must have felt sure the Angel Gabriel was either blowing that Fateful Finale of his, or was warming up for it. It was an incomparable concert.

Realizing what we had done—I take the blame for the idea—we fell back bursting with giggles while someone whispered, "Turn off the lights so they won't know where Gabriel is staying." We shook hands farewell and I scurried down before the hotel manager could discern where the hullabaloo originated. But interestingly enough, apparently no one thought that Gabriel was appearing at the Hotel Wooten, so when I went to work next day, expecting at least some inquiring phone calls, I heard never a word of the episode. Could the devout have been too disappointed to talk about it?

I still have, and play occasionally, two or three LPs containing tracks of the Four Freshmen blending the brass. I wish I could live it again.

You're Hearing—George Shearing

*I*n my period as Amusements Editor of the newspaper in Abilene, I found that if I wished, I could be busy every night covering a concert, some dramatic production or another, or viewing a new film—a little more activity than a one-man department really needed—but all of which I was expected to review. As a matter of fact, my wife, who generally accompanied me when my artsy career began, finally reached the conclusion that she could take off no more than one, maybe two, nights a week from motherhood and housewifery to go with me. She had been a reporter for the *Reporter-News* when we married and later was editor of the Women's Section, so she sympathized with hectic newspaper schedules. Therefore, with this understanding, a good bit of my critical coverage was done alone.

But no matter how I might look back on that job with a coating of amused cynicism, I greatly enjoyed being an "all-everything" critic. (I once wrote a whimsical how-to article for *Atlantic Monthly* using that title.) I think this spasm of enjoyment used to be true for most journalists on most journalistic assignments, and publishers and managing editors recognized this joy-in-the-job and took advantage of it.

Abilene had always been a little cultural oasis in the long, vacant stretches of West Texas—600 miles from Fort Worth "Where the West Begins" to El Paso, where Texas ends, with Abilene about one-third the way. Some of the other West Texas cities thought Abilene took its culture a little too seriously. While not a spokesman for culture, for better or for worse, I became the person whose thoughts on

George Shearing

public performances were the first impressions the city got.

I believe I was pretty fair in my criticism. A Chicago newspaper man named Robert Casey wrote several books about the so-called *Front Page* days of newspapering, and in one he quoted a paragraph on reporting that became my yardstick for criticism of all kinds: Reward no friends, punish no enemies, and grind no axes.

About the time I gained my one-man department status at the newspaper, electronic high-fidelity reproduction and stereo recording were taking over the radio and record industry. One night a rich young oilman who was in charge of entertainment at the Abilene Petroleum Club called me and told me to hurry on down to the club, that I could hear George Shearing, the blind pianist, and his group playing.

Abilene was the center for a lot of commercial petroleum activity and oil well service headquarters for an area covering several hundred square miles. This was in the prime of the oil business in West Texas and the local Petroleum Club was as elegant as any in the state, occupying its own wing in a local hotel. The West Texas oilmen of the 1950s were a sophisticated lot, well educated, coming from all over the United States—or, all over the world.

I was not a member of the Petroleum Club (God wot!) but I was no stranger. I had been a guest there several times and had visited with Harry James when he and a road band were playing there. (Harry James and my mother were both born in Beaumont, Texas, at about the same time.) This night when I got to the club the rich young oil-man (RYO) met me outside in the hallway. Motioning me to follow quietly, he opened the door but held me in the foyer of the club. "Hear that?" he asked, motioning toward the sound. "Isn't he great?"

I heard the unmistakable tones of the Shearing outfit and was both pleased and puzzled: how had George Shearing managed to slip into town, even at the exclusive Petroleum Club, and me not know it? I asked, "How did this happen?" and the RYO laughed, pulled me into the club's fancy bar, and there stood two huge speakers throbbing with the Shearing's piano sound—from a stereo recording.

I tried to come up with a rapid cover for my confusion, but I was obviously fooled. The RYO had told some of his fellow members he could "get to Greene," as he put it, with the new stereo system, and when he succeeded we had a good laugh, plus drinks, on the proposition. But that's not the end of the story.

A few months later this same young oilman, who was very likeable and well connected (by inheritance), called me again, urging me to come on down and hear some more George Shearing. I grumbled that I was sufficiently impressed by the club's sound system, but he added that he would furnish me with dinner and drinks—and the Petroleum Club had the finest chef in seventeen counties. My wife being out of town, I cancelled (in my mind) a movie I was thinking about going to see and went instead to the club. Once again I was met in the hallway and once again was taken to the foyer to hear the sounds of George Shearing. But this time, as you may already have guessed, I entered the bar and there sat George Shearing and group, making the musical sounds only Shearing and his accompanists could make.

Shearing himself was a quiet, genial gentleman, with a soft British accent who didn't hesitate to join any conversation that might come up, even with a small town music critic. It happened that I had a rea-sonably large amount of his music in my vocabulary and during the break he told me stories about a number of his recordings and I told him about my "George Shearing" experience of a few months before. The dinner, the drinks—he didn't eat but did have a mild drink—and the talk were superb.

Later the RYO said he had paid for Shearing's appearance out of his own pocket, just for the chance to confound me, the newspaper critic. I told him, "That's what I call the power of the press!"

The Judge Holds Court

*I*n Abilene from time to time I covered a trial, although seldom anything bigger than municipal or j.p. court. However, if you want some juicy cases—sometimes involving your friends and neighbors—these courts are where you find them. I covered the misdemeanor trial of a famous musician for stealing hubcaps, one of a fellow reporter (female) for petty theft, the *nolo contendere* of a southern governor in Abilene for a convention who gave a call girl a bad check, and an embarrassing municipal trial of a woman I knew who was charged with prostitution when a cop caught her performing fellatio on a man (not her husband) in the back seat of an auto parked on a downtown street. She (and the man) were let off with fifty dollar fines "for public exposure" when it could not be proved she had been paid for her services—or "for your job" as the municipal judge referred to the event.

By not covering the higher courts, I missed a lot of good court stories, I suppose, but I also avoided having to listen, day after day, to witnesses who were willing to lie concerning the whereabouts of the defendant at the time of the crime, or vowing the honesty of someone who would steal the rings off your fingers while you were shaking hands with him (or her)!

Of course, it wasn't always the defendant who confused things. At one routine trial I happened to sit in on, a man was seeking damages for a leg injury and there was an amusing, but awkward, mixup. The lawyer representing the plaintiff was named Dallas Scarborough. He was famous for his courtroom dramatics, and his high rate of success. Watching him had become a form of civic entertainment. I knew him, and that was why I was present in the first place; I heard Dallas Scarborough was performing.

He always carried a huge white handkerchief which he would whip out, like a flag, to wipe his face, or his tears, at the climax of his summary to the jury. Getting down on the knees to plead wasn't totally unknown, either. He was a classic of his kind. I have been challenged when I tell Scarborough stories: "There was a lawyer like that in our town and I've heard the same story about him." My answer is, "Maybe he learned it from Dallas."

One expert witness he often used was Dr. Black, a physician who was capable of giving impressive medical testimony on the spur of the moment. This trial I observed was a minor one. All he had to do was prove his client had indeed injured a leg through carelessness of another person. The defense lawyer, hired by the insurance company, had faced Dallas Scarborough before and probably would have settled had Dallas not had an unlikely figure in mind.

The only witness Scarborough put on the stand, besides an ambulance driver, was Dr. Black. The doctor made an imposing figure, oozing respect and responsibility. In the courtroom was a light box on which x-ray negatives could be mounted. Dr. Black opened the large envelope which he carried and inserted the x-ray pictures with a flourish. Using a pointer, he explained, in medical terms, the terrible injury this poor fellow's leg had suffered. The jury strained forward, trying to look intelligent as the medical man pointed out areas of abnormality, and announced it was questionable that the man would walk again—"to the extent he once enjoyed locomotion."

On cross-examination the defense attorney arose with what appeared to be a show of humility.

"Dr. Black," he said, "I won't insult you by demanding you give your medical credentials."

Dr. Black gave a small smile. "Thank you for your consideration," he said.

"But," the defense attorney continued, "I want you once again to show the jury the x-ray picture you have so carefully explained, and specify which leg is pictured."

The doctor pronounced, "Why . . . the leg pictured is the right leg."

The defense attorney, addressing the doctor but looking at the jury, said in a voice tinged with sarcasm, "But, Dr. Black, the injured leg is alleged to be the left one!"

It was like a courtroom scene from the movies: the jury looking as if some witness had introduced a box of hornets, Dallas Scarborough on his feet objecting, and Dr. Black staring at the light box. Dallas called for a recess, conferred with his opponent, and managed to get a settlement—but a much smaller settlement. As they left the courthouse, with me eavesdropping behind them, Dr. Black, handing over the x-ray packet, growled, "Dallas, you never told me which damn leg was supposed to be hurt. Don't ever do me that way again!"

★ ★ ★

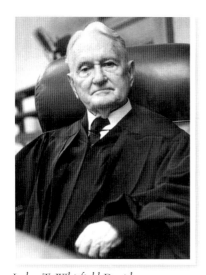

One hot summer day our man on the federal beat came down with an appendicitis attack during a session in federal circuit court and I was drafted to take his place. I had no interviews or assignments outside the office that day so I was working in my shirt sleeves, but before I went out the door for the federal courthouse another reporter warned me to wear a coat, that Judge T. Whitfield Davidson, of Dallas, was on the bench and he demanded reporters wear a coat in his courtroom. Judge Davidson was age eighty-two at the time and famed among lawyers for his despotism—although I didn't know this.

Judge T. Whitfield Davidson

I borrowed a seersucker jacket that had been hanging in the men's closet for a couple of months and walked to the courthouse. I checked in with the bailiff and made my way to the press table to take over my predecessor's notes.

I sat doodling—it was not an exciting case—when suddenly Judge Davidson slammed down his gavel and demanded, "Bailiff, who is that man?" He indicated me.

The bailiff, a big redhaired fellow, said, "Your honor, he is with the Abilene newspaper. Their other man took sick."

Judge Davidson said to the bailiff, "Bailiff, tell that man that in my court reporters wear a tie."

The bailiff acknowledged the judge's order and came over to the press table and whispered, "You heard Judge Davidson. In this court you wear a tie." I whispered back that I certainly would put on a tie as soon as possible, that due to the emergency nature of my assignment I had not been prepared to be in federal court.

The trial proceeded for a few more minutes when suddenly Judge Davidson again slammed down his gavel and said, "Bailiff . . . remove that man." He meant me.

The bailiff again approached me and said, "You have to leave. Right now." I protested I was covering the trial. "But you don't have a tie on and Judge Davidson says throw you out." The bailiff was certainly big enough to do it, especially under the circumstances. I asked if I returned wearing a tie could I get back in? The bailiff said he thought so, that the judge was a fair man.

Unconvinced of the latter proposition, I slunk from the courtroom, not sure what to do. I didn't need another tie but I had to finish the assignment. I went to the Walgreen drugstore across the street from the federal building, and lo, a miracle: there, overflowing a big plastic bowl, was a display of neckties, priced at twenty-nine cents each. I grabbed up one, paying no mind to color or design, but when I started to put it on discovered it was a boy's tie—a little boy's tie—not only much too short but with a design of tricycles and sleds. Return to court wearing this and the judge might hold me in contempt.

The Walgreen's clerk, watching my predicament, said, "Why don't you wear it like a bow tie?" I admitted I couldn't tie a bow tie. "Well, here . . . let me do it," she said. She twisted and turned the fabric and finally announced her satisfaction. "There, look at it in this mirror," she said, handing me a small mirror from beneath the counter. I studied the tie and told her it was worthy of Oscar Wilde himself. She didn't know Oscar Wilde, she said, but she had to tie bow ties for her high school age sons; her husband thought bow ties were sissy.

I returned to the courtroom of Judge T. Whitfield Davidson wearing my flowing bow tie and my borrowed seersucker jacket. I conferred with the bailiff. We waited until Judge Davidson noticed me. A quick glance and he nodded acceptance. I finished the day intact and after telling my story to the Managing Editor, tried to get him to refund the twenty-nine cents I paid for the tie. He looked at it and refused.

But that was not the last I saw of Judge T. Whitfield Davidson in action. I never covered another trial in his court, but in 1961 when, nearing age eighty-five, he delivered the final Dallas school desegregation ruling, I was there.

Judge Davidson had first heard the desegregation case the summer before, and it was not difficult to predict his ruling. He was one of the last of those unreconstructed Southern rebels who, protected by a federal judgeship, didn't have to care what they ruled or said.

After hearing the Dallas plaintiffs, Judge Davidson had rendered a long, nineteenth century peroration on the benefits of slavery, the loyalty of "the Negro" to his old master and his old mistress, how the slaves despised Emancipation, and the terrible dangers of "amalgamation," which would, of course, be brought on by school desegregation—therefore, he denied the plaintiffs' suit and called for something he termed "voluntary" desegregation.

The Court of Appeals reversed the decision (all those old arguments had been struck down) and sent it back to Judge Davidson with a "stop the nonsense" ruling: order the desegregation of the Dallas schools. Al Hester, the federal beat reporter for the *Dallas Times Herald* told me everyone knew Judge Davidson was going to have to make the desegregation order and the occasion should be historic. Thurgood Marshall, the U. S. Solicitor General (later the first black Supreme Court justice), would be present for this "victory" of integration forces.

I sat at the press table which happened to be near where Thurgood Marshall and the plaintiffs' lawyers were seated. When His Honor Judge T. Whitfield Davidson entered the crowded courtroom, I nervously checked to be certain I had on a tie.

The old judge, his mind seeming to recall a time closer to his birth in 1876 than to 1961, began by declaring, "Never have we at any time entertained one unkind thought toward the colored race. My wet nurse as a child was a Negro woman." (Thurgood Marshall flinched.) Then, despite calling desegregation "un-American" and declaring outsiders "understand not our problems as we do," the judge made the ruling: the Dallas schools would be integrated the next school year. But he warned the plaintiffs: "You are fully aware of having won in the courts of the land a history-making legal battle. If it calls for a triumph, remember the precept of General Grant at Appomattox: 'Never crow over the reverses of an honorable adversary.'"

As the hearing adjourned I watched Thurgood Marshall. He had an ordinary yellow pencil with which he had been taking notes. Shaking his head wearily, he stood up, snapped the pencil in two, and threw up the pieces exclaiming, "That man . . . that man!"

T. Whitfield Davidson left the bench in 1965 at age eighty-nine, the oldest federal judge in the U. S. He died in 1974 at age ninety-seven.

A Tall Texan's Tale

*S*ometime in 1956 or 1957 the Abilene Civic Music association signed for a future concert by the emerging young Texas pianist, Harvey Lavan Cliburn, Jr., of Kilgore. Van, as he was called, already had made appearances with the Houston Symphony (at age thirteen), the Dallas Symphony, the New York Philharmonic and had done a successful national tour. But all this was as nothing to the international acclaim that followed when in 1958 he won first prize in the most important piano competition in the world, the International Tschiakovsky Piano Competition in Moscow. This happened at a time when the U. S. and the U.S.S.R were engaged not just in a Cold War of arms, but a war of culture, and Russia was considered to have a headlock on international piano greatness. Yet here came a tall Texas pianist, age twenty-three, playing Tschiakovsky's Piano Concerto #1 before a Russian audience and Russian judges in Moscow, walking off with the top trophy of the absolute top keyboard meet. The world, not just the United States, of a sudden, went wild—Moscow most of all.

Well, Van Cliburn never made that Abilene concert, but with a good reason. Following his Tschaikovsky Competition triumph, he played the pianoforte so much (and shook hands so often, he later told me) he developed a felon—an infection of the tissue of the top joint of one of his fingers. He had to cancel all his concert dates for the coming season. The danger that this abscess would ruin his career was distinct. One day, a couple of months later, my friend Raymond Thomason, the owner and manager of the Sands Motel in Abilene—a

Van Cliburn, and his mother, Rildia Cliburn
with Russian conductor Kirill Knodchin.

glittery new place inspired by Las Vegas—called that the Cliburn
family was coming to the Sands. I telephoned the Cliburn home in
Kilgore and asked if I could meet and interview Van. His mother,
Rildia (who conducted his business with as much skill as the highest
priced agent) suggested I wait to see if he felt like it. When I called
the motel on the date their rooms were reserved, Rildia Cliburn graciously invited me to have breakfast "with us" the next morning. "Us"
included her and her husband, Harvey, and Van. Both Mr. and Mrs.
Cliburn were devoted to their son and he seemed to return their fer-
vor. He said then, and I believe he held steadfastly to the opinion,
that his mother, who was herself well trained, had been his first and
most important piano teacher.

He showed me the felon-ish finger and displayed the method of
shaking hands another concert artist had taught him: sliding the fingers so they are not crushed on one another. Van Cliburn, a large
man, not of a delicate cast, had often been the target of those guys
who seem to think they lessen their masculinity if they don't break a
bone or two when they clamp down on a celebrity's hand. As the dining room began to fill with more breakfast eaters, several recognized

the pianist's famous mop of curly hair and came over to speak a word to him. After explaining why he didn't shake hands, Van introduced his mother and father and me, without pointing out my role. As most of these people were not from the Abilene area, I'm sure they thought I had undue importance, such as being his agent or lawyer.

Our breakfast consisted pretty much of what is (too-cutely) called "down home" food—eggs, grits, ham—that sort of thing. Rildia Cliburn assured me she did a better job on grits, for example, than the chef. (Even today, few cooks outside the Deep South understand there is more to making grits than merely boiling water. This, unfortunately, includes West Texas.) Knowing how important she had been to Van's career, I had somehow expected Mrs. Cliburn to be a "stage mother" type, but she wasn't at all. She had a great deal of deep East Texas and northern Louisiana charm and mannerisms—terms understood automatically by Texans—which she retained unto her death at age ninety-six. Harvey, the father, did not sit by quietly admiring his wife and son; he took every opportunity to tell his own stories and make his own comments. This seemed a proud, happy family.

When the famous felon finger was at last pronounced well, Van Cliburn again scheduled a concert tour in our section. One of the local workers called me and said that Mr. Cliburn was to appear in San Angelo, nearly 100 miles from Abilene, and if I wished tickets he would make sure they were held at the door. My wife and I and Raymond Thomason went to San Angelo for the concert and met Van Cliburn back stage when it was finished. Amidst the press of well wishers, autograph seekers and media interviewers, I introduced Van Cliburn to my wife, instructing her on how to shake hands, a la Cliburn, to his amusement. He was quite cordial, but it was already evident that Van Cliburn was becoming more than just a harried celebrity, he was becoming that cliché, "a legend in his own time."

★ ★ ★

In the years that followed, his status in the music world never declined. His recording of the Tschiakovsky Piano Concerto #1 became the best selling classical recording in history. The Van Cliburn Piano Competition, held every fourth year in Fort Worth, replaced the Tschiakovsky Competition of Moscow in piano competition importance.

Sometime in the 1960s, when Van Cliburn gave a Dallas concert at the Fair Park Music Hall, my wife and I attended, and afterward splurged by going to Mario's, a four-star restaurant, for a late supper. Partway through our meal there was a bustle at Mario's front entrance, and half a dozen waiters flew to a table near ours setting up for a party. In came Van Cliburn and four or five others. We heard Van order a large steak and a baked potato—no, no salad and no other vegetables. After a while he called the waiter over and ordered the same meal again. He had worked hard that evening. It is my observation that pianists, violinists and symphony conductors—in that order—work harder during a concert than any other musical artists.

As my wife and I left the restaurant, we stopped by the Cliburn table. I re-introduced myself and wife, and said we had met a few years back and that I had had breakfast with him and his parents in Abilene. He said, "Of course." I was careful, shaking his hand, to use only the most delicate pressure, honored that he extended that valuable set of digits at all.

Robbity Bob's Last Concert

Few of us will admit we are wanting to become famous, or that any single act or gesture is done with fame in mind, but the only person we are kidding is ourself. Fame is the spur, says Milton, but Fame is not always a matter of success or application of skill. Becoming famed can be a matter of trying to climb a perilous glass mountain, or discovering yourself atop the peak after one giant step. But fame is as individually defined as is beauty, and no matter how frequently the mirror on the wall says you're beautiful or tells you you're famous, the mirror alone never satisfies you.

No need to repeat the trite (by now) observation that in the future everyone will be world-famous for fifteen minutes, as if it should take that much fame to satisfy anyone. The late Andy Warhol made three misassumptions in pronouncing this prophesy: sticking in "future," "world" and "fifteen minutes." He used too broad a scope. Your face flashed on-screen for a nanosecond via an audience shot at a daytime

TV show will do. (Mama, look! look! Ain't that Livinia?)

Fame is happiness, we decide: what more could Marilyn Monroe, beautiful and famous, have wanted out of life, we ask, as though her life was something we would gladly swap our own for. Fame can be tragic, as Marilyn Monroe (and hundreds like her) have proved.

What I am leading up to is another kind of tragedy involving fame: the tragedy of the pursuer who recognizes that run as hard or as fast as he may, fame will never be his. Who defines the fame he pursues? Is it world fame, fame within a certain profession, or fame in a province? Fame is in the mirror, and the mirror talks only to you, and when you see the slightest blemish, you realize the mirror lied when it told you, "You are famous!"

This is about a performer, a very good, very talented performer, who, in the hunt for recognition, had ridden a fine, spirited horse and ridden him well; had cleared the nastiest hedges and hurdles without a spill and been in at the kill, but when the trophy was awarded, when fame panned the crowd for faces: it missed him.

He had been offered by some community concert agency or another in his first tour. Abilene's Civic Music group probably scheduled him as its final performer because his fee fit what was left of that year's budget. He was young, his head-shot was handsome, and there were enough testimonials of his talent to assure the public he wouldn't embarrass any sponsorship. And, of course, in the back of the minds of such sponsorships is the possibility that this one, young, using new wings, will turn out to be the next immortal.

He was a pianist, Juilliard graduate, and had played in several U. S. and Canadian cities. I found his concert exhilarating and I especially liked the way he introduced each of his numbers in person, regardless of the fact we had printed programs furnished. There was a touch of eager appreciation for the people who had come to hear him play—*him*, not some international name. *Him*! I called in a most enthusiastic review of the young pianist, pointing out that in addition to his keyboard skill and interpretive talent, he seemed to make friends with the audience, to be genuinely glad to be playing in Abilene, Texas. I didn't count the house in print and compare him with other pianists or predict certain greatness, but I did offer the thought that his personality seemed to emerge with his music stronger than that of many more famous artists.

There was no after-concert party planned for this young player, Robert M. When I called in my review I saw an automobile sitting at the rear entrance of the auditorium and, recognizing the driver as husband of one of the Civic Music sponsors, I asked if he were waiting for Robert. He said, "Yeah" that his wife had "suggested" he take "this guy" back to his hotel. I could see that the driver was perhaps a better husband than a music lover, so I volunteered to haul the young man myself, "In fact," I said, "I may take him to supper." "Ever' place worth eatin' at'll be closed down," the husband noted, but I said I thought I could find a late-night spot, and the would-be driver sped off, relieved to be going home and so to bed, I suppose.

I found the young pianist coming down the hall from the dressing rooms, introduced myself again (I had visited very briefly backstage before his concert), and after explaining about the other vehicle, asked if I could take him to supper. "I am delighted," he said, "and hungry." He was very likeable, with a bit more humor about him than I had found in most artists. I was not a member of the Petroleum Club but did have an informal permit to bring guests there when they were visitors of importance. "Open saloons," that dear old pre-Prohibition term, were outlawed in Texas but private clubs could operate pretty much the same as a saloon. By this hour the Petroleum Club was exceptionally private; there were only three or four members in the bar, there was another table of diners, and a weekly poker game was going on in one of the side rooms. I laughed and asked Robert if he were old enough to drink and he answered, "Only something mild, like a double dry martini."

I told him how much I enjoyed his concert, and I assured him this was personal, not just journalistic hogwash. "You have some exciting something that comes through when you play," I told him. "I look forward to hearing your recordings," and I added that I'd said as much in my review.

"God, I appreciate that," he said. "Some places I'm lucky if they even mention this 'piano player' in the local paper. I told my manager, I wish I was a foot taller or sixty pounds heavier so I could bill myself as an ex-basketball player in the midwest and 'former football star' in the southwest."

During the meal he told me how grateful he was that I had asked him out (as he put it). "You know," he shook his head rather sadly, "at my level you don't get rich on tour." He took a sip of the wine we were having and said, "I've had a hamburger and a Coke—alone—after more than one concert. My contract doesn't specify four-star meals."

The wine kept coming and after Robert's double martini (double dry and double size) the effects were evident in the jovial mood in which he insisted we both refer to him as "Robbity-Bob." He held up the remains of a glass of wine and announced solemnly: "Here's to Robbity-Bob on his last concert."

Assuming he meant this was the last stop on his tour, I held my glass to his and said something about " . . . and here's to the next one," or the like. But he shook his head in denial.

"I said 'last' and I meant last. This was the last concert I'll ever play on the last tour I'll ever make."

"Come on, Robert," I said, "there's a great future in front of you."

He waved an admonitory finger at me, "'Robbity-Bob', not Robert. Robbity-Bob is what I am. Robert's too formal. Famous men are named Robert. Nobody famous is named Robbity-Bob."

I felt sure the wine was doing most of the talking; I wasn't too steady myself. I laughed at his "Robbity-Bob" routine and even joined him in singing as we made up rhymes to it:

Robbity-Bob is a hopeless slob . . . or, can't
get a job . . . or, too poor to rob but isn't a snob.

Then I noticed the tears, and knew they weren't from the wine.

I said, "Robert's no different from Robbity-Bob and Robbity-Bob is great." I held off a second, seeing my speech wasn't going in. "You'll feel better after you've rested up. You said yourself, this tour's been brutal."

He didn't try to wipe off the tears. "No, I'm through. I missed my shot."

"Hasn't this been a successful tour? You were telling me about how the Canadians touted you in Calgary or Edmonton, or whatever city."

"That's because of my last name. They thought I was Scotch."(I have not used that name, but it was one of the Mac- or Mc- variety.)

"But one tour can't do all that to you. Can't you keep touring, getting better and better dates and then a recording contract?"

"Sure," he said, "I can stay with it—and always be the last artist on the Abilene Civic Music program. Maybe even be the first some year when they can't get anyone famous until the second month. But recording contract? Better and better tour dates? Not a chance."

I kept protesting. I hoped it was a matter of giving him courage. "You've been well received. Look at the crowd tonight. You've gotten rave reviews . . . mine, for instance."

He gave me a smile, "A. C., you're not what counts." He stopped, waiting to explain, but I understood, and nodded agreement.

"St. Louis and Denver and Richmond aren't what count. Maybe even New York. The competition isn't just in the U. S. The best pianist in the world may come from Texas—we had discussed Van Cliburn—but he has to convince Europe first."

"But Robby . . . you've got so much talent, it seems like a shame just to give up and waste it."

"I'm not 'giving up.' I'm just recognizing facts: I'm not going to be a great concert pianist. Nobody has come to me with a recording contract; nobody has asked me to play with the Philadelphia or the Boston or New York Philharmonic . . . I'm not going to make it."

How was I to tell him to stay with it, to keep on keeping on—all those wonderful "little engine that could" stories?

"What about your piano?" I asked. "Can't you continue to play?"

He laughed, not quite from amusement. "I'm not going to end up scrounging for bucks at some piano bar."

I tried to lighten the moment. "Why not? I'll request 'Little Girl Blue'—and you can sing it. You've got a great piano bar voice."

Robbity-Bob contemplated. "Jesus, you know, I can't even do that. I can't take requests unless they're by Chopin or Liszt. I've never studied anything but classical piano."

His sigh was elemental: "I've given my life to the piano. I haven't even dated a girl who wasn't a piano student, or was at least in music school."

"What would you like to do, if you give up concertizing?"

He waited. "You know what I'd really like to do? I'd like to get married, live in some small town, maybe like this one. Have friends like you and your wife. Have you over for chicken on the grill, or hamburgers and beer."

"And give up music altogether?"

"Oh, no . . . not that. But . . ."

"But what?"

"But never play the piano except when I am by myself, when nobody can say to me, 'Gee, you're pretty good. You ought to be on th' concert circuit.'"

The Petroleum Club was closing; one by one the bar-flies left the club, the other table of diners had departed quite a while before, and when the poker players came out, full of tobacco smoke and not altogether shared laughter, I signed the check and Robbity-Bob and I left, too. In the car, as I took him back to his hotel, he sat singing over and over the rhymes we had made, "Robbity-Bob has lost his job, the helpless slob . . . ."

When my review of his concert appeared I had several people tell me they would have attended if they had thought it was going to be as good as I reported it to be . . . it was just that they'd never heard of him, and you know how you are sometimes . . .

I treasure the dramatic and soulful head-shot his artists' agency sent out. Before we left the club, Robert signed it thusly:

> *To Brother A.C., whose efforts to further my career*
> *failed utterly and ignominiously—*
>
> > *Balefully,*
> > *Robbity-bob*

An Attempt to Kill Segovia

When Andrés Segovia, the celebrated Spanish guitarist, died, I was deeply effected by emotions of grief and guilt. I have been accused of trying to kill him and despite the passage of time, I haven't forgiven myself. Why in the world would you try to kill Segovia, someone is asking, knowing that he was a fine, inoffensive artist?

Andrés Segovia

Were you jealous because you knew nothing about the instrument? Had you inferred a slighting reference when listening to his music? Of course not. I didn't intentionally try to kill Andrés Segovia.

The episode took place in the late 1950s, when I was the one-man entertainment staff of the Abilene newspaper. The Civic Music committee, which annually brought four or five musical artists to Abilene, asked me for help in planning a future season. When I saw that it might be possible to bring Andrés Segovia, I said immediately, "There is my nomination." I was in awe of Segovia. I had several LPs and tapes of his solos and I found they offered the most soothing yet inspiring music by which to work. One especial favorite of mine was an Edvard Grieg piece based on a Norwegian folk melody that Segovia made to sound nothing at all like Norway and altogether like Spain.

Segovia's appearance was to be in the auditorium of Hardin-Simmons University. The night of the performance one of the hostesses leading the music series asked me if I would stay backstage as she was unfamiliar with this particular auditorium and I had at one time taught at this school. I, of course, agreed.

Señor Segovia spoke only moderate English but was very gracious when I attempted to talk to him in my schoolboy Spanish just before curtain time. I asked ("por favor") if he would be able to play the Grieg melody ("la melodía Grieg") and he said he would "if requested to play an encore," as his selections were already printed on the program. I felt certain there would be encores, so I was satisfied.

Shortly after that, only moments before he was supposed to begin playing, Sr. Segovia asked if it would be possible for him to obtain a drink of water. The woman in charge came to me and asked if I could locate water for the guest, and do so rapidly. I took the plastic cup she offered and went searching backstage, down a long corridor facing the dressing rooms. It was dimly lit, in the tradition of backstage areas, and as soon as I saw a faucet I filled the cup, ran back to the maestro and gave him the water. He hurriedly gulped it down just as the curtain was rising.

Seated in a plain wooden chair with one foot elevated on a small wooden box which he brought along, he patiently waited for the introductory applause to die down. But just before his first chord I could hear him mumbling, "Muerte . . . todos mueren . . . death . . . they all die . . ." or so it sounded to me. I couldn't imagine what I was hearing. Surely he wasn't wishing disaster on our city. His acceptance had been all but boisterous, and he had been very much the fine old Spanish gentleman with the hostesses and me, so I knew it must be my hearing or my hesitant Spanish that had fashioned this off-key remark. But for the next two numbers I continued to hear, very faintly, from my hiding place onstage behind the curtain, "They die . . . ." Then, on my knees so as to get the best hearing angle I could, I eventually made out a sentence, "Beben las aguas . . . mueren. They drink this water, they die!"

Then it began to make better sense to me. The water in our town was pure and clean, but at certain times of the year, when the municipal lake "turned over," we citizens were told, the taste could be rather unpleasant. Residents became used to it but visitors didn't, so that told me what Andrés Segovia was mumbling about: he couldn't see how the people of this town survived drinking this water.

At the intermission, Sr. Segovia again asked for water. The same woman came to me with another, larger cup and asked me, once again, to bring the maestro a drink.

"He said something about hoping he didn't die from the water," the woman said, rather puzzled. "Was he joking?" I told her my theory of the lake turning over and causing the water to "taste" as it did. She nodded, but wasn't really convinced, I could tell.

Hastening back down the dim hallway to the water outlet, I reached to turn the handle, and discovered what I had not discovered before: the handle, which looked innocent enough, was giving water from a folded fire hose. I had given Andrés Segovia, the world's finest guitarist, water that had been sitting in a rubber-lined fire hose for, I suppose, months.

Horrified at what I had done, I did not even try to find a drinking fountain but climbed out a backstage window, raced across the street to the university's student center, and obtained a big cup of pure water, with ice. Bolting through the same low window, I came back to the dressing room where the hostess was fidgeting nervously but was too glad to see me to remonstrate with me for my tardiness. I thrust the plastic cup into her hands, saying, "Here. Maybe this won't kill him!" She looked at me with mild astonishment but took the precious water to Sr. Segovia, and throughout the rest of his program he hummed contentedly as he played, never dreaming that some stranger in this Texas town had maybe tried to kill him ("intento de asesinato").

And for his first encore he played my Grieg melody, smiling back at me as he did.

An Incidental Academic Introduction

Although I had once planned to become a public school teacher, my heart was never really in the profession after I took the course "Fundamentals of Educational Psychology" my first year in college. But on getting my B.A. in 1948, I started to Salida, Colorado, to be interviewed for a high school teaching position. Jobs in Texas were hard to find for a certificateless history major, but Salida was willing to suspend such technical requirements.

My automobile, a 1927 Rolls Royce Phantom II, which I had spotted in Dallas while delivering Coca-Cola (and for which I had paid $275), changed my mind about teaching and got me into the newspa-

Larry McMurtry and Robert Duvall,
an epic "chance encounter" for both.

per business. Here is how it happened. As I was driving it from Dallas to Salida, it seemed to me it needed its brakes repaired. To save money, I found a mechanic in Abilene who said he'd work on it "when he got time," and three weeks later discovered the vehicle only had rear-wheel brakes. Within that time I had been forced to find a temporary job which led me into the newspaper business—so I didn't make it to Salida or into high school teaching.

But one night in 1957 at the annual banquet of the Abilene Chamber of Commerce, a man who introduced himself as Dr. Elwin Skiles, president of Hardin-Simmons University, asked me if I would come out to his office Monday. He thought I would make a splendid chair(man) for the Journalism Department. I told him I had no teaching certificate, but he said a certificate was not necessary to teach at the university level.

That was how I got into teaching. I didn't stay long that first time but I enjoyed it once I discovered it wasn't like the education course books had made it seem. I spent the next thirty years mostly in the newspaper, radio or television business and writing books, teaching at the University of Texas at Austin and at Southern Methodist University for brief periods.

In 1985 when my wife and I were at a book publication party for Larry L. King, the *Best Little Whorehouse* playwright, Dr. James Ward Lee, of North Texas State University, told me of plans to establish The Center for Texas Studies at that school. "I think it sounds like your kind of thing," he said. So, in 1986 I was hired as "Resident Professor of Texas Studies," a handmade title.

A few months after I joined the faculty the school (now University of North Texas) began celebration of a major literary gathering which Jim Lee had put together called "The Governor's Conference on Texas Literature." (The "Governor" part of the title was misleading. Texas Governor Mark White had promised $25,000 toward the conference, but at the last minute—too late to change the printed posters and such—he backed out. Politics?)

The conference brought together a most complete set of Texas writers—poets, novelists, playwrights, essayists—known and just beginning. This included such stars as the elusive William Humphreys, playwright Horton Foote, John Graves, Harryette Mullen, Larry McMurtry (who had gotten his B.A. from North Texas), and Jim Lehrer of television news fame. The entire three-day event was well attended by students and the public, and even the writers—sometimes a sullen bunch—enjoyed the conference and each other.

The gathering offered more than just writers, however. There were not only film scripters. There were directors, agents and players, including Robert Duvall, fresh from his starring role in Horton Foote's Academy Award winning *Tender Mercies*. Duvall stepped back into his *Tender Mercies* movie persona one afternoon and sang western songs with a musical group of professors known as "The East Texas String Ensemble" (pronounced "strang in-symbol").

The second night the university and the Texas Institute of Letters gave a party for all the participants. A lavish buffet was laid out and one of the famous North Texas jazz bands played for dancing or listening. I was standing at one end of the darkened ballroom when I noticed Robert Duvall nearby, alone for the moment. I told him how impressive he had been in *Tender Mercies* and I asked him if he had been born in Texas, his Texas accent was so good, but he said no. However, he implied his parents had lived in the Lone Star State, but further explained, "I spent a week learning to sharpen my Texas accent in the best place possible—Abilene, Texas." I exclaimed that I had been born and raised in Abilene but hadn't thought of it as the epicenter of a Texas accent. "Well," he said, "you've sure got one yourself."

While we were talking about Abilene and West Texas and Duvall's acting, I noticed Larry McMurtry standing a few feet away, and I motioned for him to join us. I had known him since his first novel, *Horseman, Pass By* which was made into *Hud*. He had also written *The Last Picture Show* and *Terms of Endearment* which, like *Hud*, won Academy Awards. He had just scored a critical success with his newest book, *Lonesome Dove*, but it had not yet been awarded the Pulitzer Prize. I introduced Larry and Robert Duvall who knew of each other but had not met. I mentioned that Larry's *Lonesome Dove*, was an exciting novel and I told Duvall it was his kind of book. He said he'd heard about it and was planning to get a copy. The three of us chatted for a few minutes, but these two stars were quickly surrounded by fans, so they were hustled off to another part of the forest.

Neither writer nor actor nor I realized what this chance encounter could signify later. Duvall, of course, played perhaps his greatest role as Gus in the television series based on *Lonesome Dove*, and *Lonesome Dove* may not have been McMurtry's best book—although most readers think so—but it certainly gave him the most fame, and we need not discuss money, need we?

Bidding Time With Goren

*M*ost of the famous or near-famous persons I encountered while working in West Texas were musicians or public performers of that stripe. But not all. One man of the world I encountered was Charles Goren, the creator of the Goren point-count system of bidding for contract bridge.

Taking, for a moment, a look at the game of bridge itself, I have never been able to become a good player. I think it is caused by my having played the game of poker where you can (theoretically) both bluff and win without holding great cards. In bridge you may finesse a time or two, but you can't bluff without holding the cards—and that's not bluffing.

But this isn't about poker, it's about bridge, so to return to the subject. When my late wife Betty and I first married, we made a pact that we would never play cards at the same table. It wasn't that I was good and she was unlucky—*au contraire*—she had fantastic luck at cards, consistently beating me at everything from canasta to gin rummy. Her luck hurt my pride. I wouldn't let her learn poker—for her sake.

Of course, in the matter of luck at cards, occasionally the blind sow finds an acorn, as the old southern saw says. One night, some years after my wife and I had wed, two lovely female friends named Billie and Helen staged a bridge/supper party and insisted Betty and I attend. I protested to Betty that Billie, a real expert, would embarrass me even playing bridge in the same room with her, but Betty said I was being silly, and added that she would make sure she and I didn't end up at the same table.

Overweight by thirty pounds, I was taking diet pills at that time, on a doctor's prescription. The prescribing physician was an old friend of mine and neither of us realized the potential for disaster these "feel-good" pills might hold. Sometimes the pills gave me enormous spurts of energy and a kind of synthetic bravado which translated into good will and self confidence. The pills, as you may have guessed, were "Speed," but let me quickly add, I didn't become addicted—and I lost the thirty pounds.

The night of the bridge/supper party was one of those times when I was feeling terrific. Our area was having its usual spring tornado alert, and I worked late at the newspaper office calling the telephone operators in all the little towns around to check on funnel sightings and such. (For those readers who remember operators in small towns, hasn't something gone out of life altogether since you no longer can ask "Information" to please step outside and see what the weather is or on which rural route Bob Green lives?)

I decided to walk to the party. There was only one automobile in our household and my wife was using it. The walk was a fair distance from the office, but, full of pep-pill energy, I trotted much of the way and arrived rarin' to play bridge. A rubber had already been played— the hostesses were muchly put out with me—but new partnerships

Charles Goren

were made up and play was begun on the second rubber. And guess who I drew as my partner: Billie the expert.

The first thing Billie wanted to know was, did I play Goren Point-Count? I said of course. She asked about such procedures as the Blackwood Convention and I nodded yes; Stayman Convention, of course? Of course. (I was searching my memory for the difference.) With her shaky confidence somewhat, but only somewhat, buttressed, we drew to see who would deal. Our opponents dealt and easily won the first bid. Our opponents also took the second hand, although I had tried to respond to my partner with ten or eleven points. Not enough.

Billie was a very delicate, very pretty woman, but by now she was becoming tight lipped. She was as competitive as she was delicate, and with me as her partner the future looked bleak. When the third hand was dealt, I was jolted awake by what I was holding. I saw four aces, three kings and some more face cards—I quit counting. I wasn't sure how to count it anyway. When I opened with one no trump, Billie blanched and responded with two clubs—a Stayman Convention response meaning beware, she didn't have a great deal in her hand, but (Stayman? Blackwood?) I didn't realize that was what it meant. I took her two club bid as genuine and since the king of clubs was the only king I lacked I enthusiastically responded "Four no trump!"—the diet pill coming to life again. The opponent on my left immediately doubled (which, if you are unfamiliar with bridge, means your opponent thinks you're crazy to make such a bid), and I redoubled (which means your opponent *knows* you're crazy.) If Texas had had the concealed handgun law it passed later, I would be writing this as a dead man; Billie looked everywhere for a weapon to use on me. She realized I had misinterpreted her Stayman Convention response despite having assured her I knew it.

Our opponents could scarcely conceal their delight. This was going to make amusing talk (at Billie's expense) at the next few meetings of the Abilene Duplicate Bridge Club. Billie laid down dummy's hand with an undisguised sigh of despond. But when I saw it—there was my king of clubs along with a couple of lesser face cards—I breathed again.

The opponent led a heart, I think it was. I took the trick with my king of hearts, led a small club to dummy's king of clubs, then led a small club back to my ace and, *Gott zie dank*, pulled in the queen. I laid down my hand—I couldn't be stopped. The point total for a notrump game, doubled and redoubled, along with little things like holding four aces, etc., was tremendous. About the time Billie finished adding up our score Helen announced supper was ready, so we put away the cards, cleared the tables, and served ourselves buffet. I entertained the table with stories of (possible) local scandals and the like, but Billie said hardly a word. A few mornings later, over a cup of coffee at the Grace Hotel coffee shop, Fred, her husband (who had been out of town for the game), asked me, "What happened to Billie in the bridge game the other night? She won't talk about it."

"Fred," I said, "I think I scared her so bad she *can't* talk."

And I have never played another hand of competitive bridge since that delicious night.

★ ★ ★

But back to my meeting with Charles Goren. Goren, at this time, was the biggest name in international bridge, and his point-count system had revolutionized the game.

Abilene had developed a number of good duplicate bridge players who had formed the duplicate club and made it into a serious undertaking, especially among the women, as already implied. At some point in 1958 or 1959 one of these women called and insisted I must do an interview with Charles Goren who was coming to Abilene to play with the duplicate club and give members tips on play—but mainly giving them the chance to say, "I played with Charles Goren." Maybe adding, sotto voce, "In the same room, at least."

I told my friend I recognized Goren's importance as a world figure and I agreed there should be an interview, but I wasn't the one to do it. For one thing, he didn't really fall into my territory of arts coverage, and for another, and more important reason, I was not much of a bridge player, and nowhere near the duplicate tourney level. She insisted, so I agreed, to her gracious thanks.

Charles Goren came in on a noonish plane, and I waited until about 1 o'clock to call him at the Windsor Hotel. He answered the phone himself and when I told him my wishes he hesitated, then explained, "I'm pretty weary. I flew directly here from London. Can you give me an hour to straighten up?" I said of course. "And can our meeting be for twenty minutes or less? I hate to put a time limit on you but I must rest." "By all means," I said.

When I went to the hotel I discovered Goren was in the Presidential Suite, a set of corner rooms that had been beautifully decorated by my next-door neighbor, Pat Wood. Goren answered my knock and invited me in very graciously. I assured him this interview would be quick, and we sat down. He commented on the luxurious suite, which, I'm sure, he was surprised to find in a West Texas town like Abilene.

I told him I had been in the retail book business when his *Point Count Bidding* and *Point Count Bridge Complete* were first becoming best sellers, and had sold "hundreds of them," which was a slight exaggeration, but this was no place to quote figures. I told him about my recent feat making four-no, doubled and redoubled based on not knowing the Stayman Convention. He became very genial when he discovered I was not posing as some expert, and he joked, "You've probably gotten a full hand of one suit, too, haven't you?" I said yes, playing with fellow Marines in China I had been dealt thirteen cards of the same suit.

"And I'll tell you the suit," Goren said, "spades. I've not known a person who was dealt thirteen of a suit and the suit not to have been spades." He smiled. "Somebody set it up. I've never seen a legitimate full suit hand dealt."

We talked more about bridge and how he got into the game. He said he had been, and was still, a Philadelphia lawyer, and had I ever thought about the fact that so many bridge experts were lawyers? We discussed Philadelphia for a moment, then the subject of books came up and he asked me my thoughts on W. Somerset Maugham. I expressed keen interest in Maugham, regarding him not only as a master playwright and storyteller but as a writer's writer; his autobiographies, *The Summing Up* and *A Writer's Notebook* are full of wonderful advice for writers at all levels.

"And I understand he's a good bridge player," I said. Charles Goren immediately responded: "He's one of my favorite people in the world. I was playing bridge with him last night." (That was London time.)

From that point on we talked about Maugham and books. Goren said that Maugham (Bill, he called him) was just what he (Maugham) had said he was: a good bridge player of the second rank. But that was not the reason Goren tried to play with him every time he could. Maugham was a joy to play with, making amusing comments of a cosmopolitan nature, telling stories on himself, and that second rank business still put him far ahead of most players.

Goren, of course, knew poker, and I brought up Maugham's story about the older man, an inveterate poker player, who quit the game when he won a huge pot with a spade flush, but after he'd won discovered one of the "spades" was a club. The man realized (according to Maugham) his mind was beginning to play tricks on him and in the crowd he played poker with that could be fatal.

Well, the twenty minute interview stretched closer to two hours, with me initially insisting every few minutes that I mustn't keep Mr. Goren from his nap. After an hour he and I forgot about the nap.

Now, do you want a really ironic conclusion to my bridge experiences? In 1962 I was hired to ghostwrite a paperback book titled *Instant Bridge*, a bridge system handbook which was put together from the expertise of the late Ralph Randle, Dallas bridge teacher (11,000 students), and Jim Jacoby, the son of famed card expert

Oswald Jacoby and an internationally famed player in his own right. If in doubt about my ghostly role, find a copy of *Instant Bridge* and look on page 10. The book sold a million copies.

★ ★ ★

Poker again: I have always had to restrain myself at the poker table, else I will ooch around and try and bluff far too often. I also have a hard time keeping a poker face. Not that I am a bad poker player—a pigeon—but I enjoy the game too much to hold myself back from participating. (Professionals love to hear someone talk like that.)

Beside one weekly game (friendly) at which a new participant pulled out an ugly .45 pistol and placed it on the table in front of him, I had another interesting encounter at poker which didn't make itself interesting for another twenty years. Early in my journalistic life as a sports writer, I was occasionally involved in covering Hardin-Simmons University's successful basketball program even though I was not too well prepared for the game. In that period I played nickel-ante poker now and then with some of the basketball players—games where five dollars was a fairly high bet. I have forgotten most details, other than I didn't lose. One of the poker players was a hoopster named Doyle Brunson. Imagine my surprise, many years later, to discover Doyle had become a Las Vegas gambler under the nickname "Texas Dolly" and more than once won the title "World's Champion Poker Player" in the early years of that annual Las Vegas contest. Therefore, I used to brag that, yeah, I played with the World's Champion poker player—and didn't lose.

The Richest Woman in America

Post City, Texas, was founded in 1907 as a sort of Utopian community by C. W. Post, the creator of Postum, Post Toasties, Grape-Nuts and other cereals. No liquor was to be sold in the town. Everyone was to own his own home, and farmers, Post's favored inhabitants, could buy lands (with wells, fences and some amenities in place) for reasonable prices per acre. The site was a rather featureless prairie, so trees were planted along every street and Main Street was a very wide, divided and electrically lighted boulevard. Lands were "not to be sold to speculators." A large textile mill was later opened and for years its "Postex" and "Garza" sheets and pillow cases were famous across Texas (Garza is the name of the county).

C. W. Post had earlier been successful in the Fort Worth real estate business and he invested heavily in Texas lands. He often referred to himself as a Texan, according to his daughter, Marjorie Merriweather Post.

The town of Post sits right up next to the Caprock, a twisting, turning two- or three-hundred-mile geological escarpment that lifts "The Texas High Plains" 200 feet or more above the rougher lands below. The High Plains are ideal for irrigated farming while some of the most famous ranches in Texas (the working home of the first Marlboro Man, for instance) lie in the rough lands at the foot of the Caprock.

But the agrarian prospects of Post City were hurt by a common West Texas complaint: lack of rainfall. The Cereal King spent thousands of dollars between 1910 and 1913 in the most elaborate series of experiments in U. S. rainmaking ever tried to that time. Calling them "rain battles," he had lines of cannons fired into likely looking clouds, he sent dynamite aloft by kites and balloons to explode among the clouds—when there were clouds. Alas, things worked out wet only sporadically.

The town was originally run by the Double U Land Corporation, a special entity set up by Post at his Michigan headquarters. It was not a company town, however, and Post, with "City" deleted from its name, incorporated in 1914 when population reached one thousand. The city of Post retained its loyalty to its founder, who died in 1914, and in 1957 staged a celebration for the fiftieth anniversary of the founding of C. W. Post's dream community. C. W. Post's daughter, Mrs. Marjorie Merriweather Post, agreed to come down for the celebration. Marjorie Post had married several times, so, with the addition of "Mrs.," she went back to her maiden name. Mrs. Post had taken her cereal inheritance and turned it into the General Foods Corp. In 1957 she was the richest woman in America—so rich that after her death when her heirs tried to give her lavish Florida estate to Uncle Sam, he had to debate whether to take it. He couldn't afford the upkeep.

Marjorie Post

Even though the town of Post was a little outside our circulation area, sitting nearly 140 miles to the northwest, the *Abilene Reporter-News* and I decided Mrs. Post's visit was enough to justify my using a staff car and a company gasoline credit card to drive up there.

The celebration was taking place in the wide esplanade park which lay between the Santa Fe Railway station and the (former) Algerita Hotel. I quickly found Mrs. Post and she allowed me to take her picture. She was a beautiful woman (excellent legs) in her seventieth year (I didn't ask, I looked it up), and very elegant. She was wearing a rather simple suit of light gray material with maroon piping. Her jewelry was probably costly but it was not dazzling. I can only recall a plain necklace, a wristwatch (or was it a bracelet) and a couple of rings.

She told me she had been to Texas many times, especially as a girl, with her father when he was trying to get Post City started. She had remained involved with the Post lands in Texas long after her father's death, several times helping drought-stricken farmers hold on to their farms with special loans. C. W.'s only child, she was his favorite person. He took her with him everywhere and taught her business affairs. She had been with him at the sanitorium where he had gone for treatment of a nervous disorder just before he died (a suicide, although she never accepted this.) He had divorced her mother, Ella

Letitia Merriweather, in 1904 and promptly married Marjorie's travel companion, Leila Young. Marjorie inherited the bulk of her father's huge fortune.

I asked Mrs. Post about a story I had heard, that when her husband, Joseph Davies, was named first U. S. Ambassador to the Soviet Union in 1936, she and Ambassador Davies had arrived in Communist Russia aboard his grand yacht, the "Sea Cloud." She said that was correct, and the reason they used the yacht was so they could take along plenty of food, Russian food having a bad reputation. "A man who worked for me, Mr. [Clarence] Birdseye, had invented frozen foods and we stocked the yacht's freezers with his products." She had obtained the services of Mr. Birdseye in 1929 when her Postum Corporation had bought his General Foods to form the General Foods Corporation

We were standing alongside a silvery streamlined railroad car and, being a rail buff, I asked if it was hers. She said no, that Mr. Budd [another Clarence], President of Santa Fe Railway system, had loaned her his private car to travel down. I naively said it was too bad she didn't have her own private car and for the only time in our interview she looked at me with slightly elevated eyebrow and said, "I've owned six of them."

I mentioned her daughter, the movie actress Dina Merrill, of whom she seemed quite proud, and when I asked Mrs. Post if she had ever done theater work herself she laughed and said, yes, but only in amateur theatricals, "which were very amateur." I could also tell that despite the fact she had inherited several million dollars in 1914, she felt that her "richest woman in America" status—which phrase was not mentioned, of course—was her own doing.

After about an hour, punctuated now and then by dignitary visits, a request was made that she let a group of Boy Scouts do what the leader said was an authentic "Indian dance" in her honor. She did as requested, moving into a circle of the dancing boys, all dressed in Indian garb. I think there were three or four authentic Native Americans in the troop.

I had been introduced to the man briefly, and throughout my interview with Mrs. Post her business manager had stood by, within hearing of our conversation but not participating. He was, in the business jargon of the day, the perfect "Gray Flannel Suit Man": a mature forty-five or so, a well-modulated, accentless voice, suit expensively cut, shoes of the kind with hand written numbers inside, hair neatly trimmed, a tie "rich and modest" like that of T. S. Eliot's "Prufrock." I could not help admiring the poise of this unprotesting New Yorker— Easterner, at least—in the far, hot and dry (by weather and by vote) reaches of West Texas, calmly taking everything in instead of complaining, as many visitors did: "What th' hell do people out here do for entertainment?"

When Mrs. Post went to be honored by the dancers the business manager stood by me for a few moments, observing the dancers, then asked what newspaper I represented. I told him the *Abilene Reporter-News*, adding that although our circulation was minor, compared to a metropolitan paper, the area we covered was, by contrast, immense. I said, "We're the most important newspaper between Fort Worth and El Paso."

The gray flannel suit man smiled. "You don't have to tell me about the *Reporter-News*. I used to deliver it when I was a boy. I grew up in Merkel." Merkel is a town practically within Abilene. When I told him I was born in Abilene, he began to tell me things about my hometown I didn't know. He suggested next time I was in New York I go by the office of the *New York Daily News* and meet the man who ran the newspaper, "Tex" James. "He is also from Abilene."

Just as I was about to ask how he became connected with Mrs. Post, she returned from the dance and the official Post celebrants swept everybody away. Now, passing through Post, I've often wondered if I shouldn't offer to put down some kind of plaque to mark the spot where I interviewed "The Richest Woman in America."

A Tale of a Portable Piano

*M*ost of the concert musicians I encountered as reviewer and music critic were rather good natured about performing out in the sticks, as I am sure a good many of them saw Abilene. In Abilene their music was usually more than well received; sometimes the reception was stupendous. The night the original Robert Shaw Chorale sang, the crowd called for so many encores that Robert Shaw had to come to the footlights and beg the audience's pardon: "We've run out of songs!"

When pianist Leonard Penario played Abilene, one of the hostesses who delighted in entertaining musical and stage greats, asked me if I would mind waiting for Maestro Penario, following the concert, and bring him to her home for a reception. I fairly often brought performers to parties in their honor after their concerts. I sent word backstage before Mr. Penario's concert that I was to be his driver.

As with all good musicians, appreciation brought out the finest in Leonard Penario. The audience reaction to the first part of his program was so voluble that the second portion saw him almost attacking the piano—ordinarily he was not the kind of pianist who becomes so animated. I wrote an extra long coverage of the concert, and he took a little longer to cool down and clean up, so that we were a few minutes late getting to the party. I assured him the gathering would include many knowledgeable music lovers, that Abilene was blessed with more than the usual proportion of intelligent listeners to the town's size. "However," I volunteered, "if you find yourself trapped, give me some sort of signal and I'll send a rescue squad." He laughed and said he was sure it wouldn't be necessary.

Leonard Penario's private reception proceeded smoothly, but one amusing occurrence took place, and the victim—or the perpetrator—warned me later that if I ever told it she would kill me, figuratively speaking (I trust). After more than four decades, however, I think the risk is worth taking.

When Penario and I arrived, late, as noted, there was a slight delay in the doorbell being answered. When the door was opened, our hostess appeared startled, glancing back over her shoulder—but smiling graciously. I think she might have been chiding her husband over some wifely worry and feared we had overheard it.

"Mrs. Southey," I said, "this is Leonard Penario."

Mrs. Southey beamed, "Everyone *adored* your concert. We are so honored to have you as our guest . . ." Still not inviting us in, she paused, searching for some lost chord, then looked at him helplessly: "Did you bring your piano?"

Arthur Fiedler

Nights With The Boston Pops

I think an artist's attitude toward playing a small town marks the attitude such an artist has toward humanity in general. On the artist's part, there should be a curiosity about what people want and what they might think about the arts in general—not merely what they think about the individual performer. I wouldn't want to pose as a philosopher, but doesn't it sort of hurt to discover that a great musician, for example, cares nothing about literature, or a famous painter shrugs off music? And what about critics? Must they be trained to "understand" the music or the painting they are attempting to pronounce on; should a book reviewer be specially versed in the life of or the body of criticism written about a specific author? Or should the sum of all criticism come from the simple hearing, viewing, or reading of the work at hand?

I know, I know . . . there are works of art today that are too complicated for the average viewer to see into, with the resulting "an ape could do that" viewer attitude. We hear much music that seems to edge on cacophony yet asks for serious critical acceptance. There are more and more nonfiction books written which demand foreknowledge and a presumed bias on the part of a reader.

Is a person of reasonable intelligence to be shut out of all such music, art and writing? On the other hand, can a critic be over-qualified? Philistines may bring up that worn metaphor of the monkey, the typewriter (computer?) and enough paper eventually producing the Declaration of Independence, but this is often the response of frustration at inability to respond.

But, returning to the original question about small towns and performer attitudes. For a couple of the years when I was the amusements editor, Abilene was on the circuit (I guess you'd call it) for the Boston Pops Orchestra when Arthur Fiedler, its founder, was its conductor. (I was told later, by a man who had been the business manager of several orchestras, that most of the musicians in the traveling Boston Pops were from other orchestras and were not members of the Boston Pops orchestra in Boston.)

I met Arthur Fiedler for the first time at one of the after-concert parties hostesses give for the visiting artists. Fiedler was famous for his alleged pomposity, but he certainly displayed none of it in the two years when I covered his visits. On our initial meeting he was having a drink at the bar of the party-givers' home. After I was introduced I told him I had enjoyed the show the Boston Pops put on and said I had heard the Pops several years before when they played "Deep In the Heart of Texas" and put down their instruments and clapped at the proper times. It became the classic treatment of the popular song. I asked if the Pops played the song, with sound effects, outside Texas and he laughed, "Oh, god . . . that was one of the most popular things we ever did. Played it all over America—all over the world!"

We discussed music in general and musical criticism in particular and I confessed that my main qualification for being a music critic, other than having a job on a newspaper that decided it needed an amusements editor, was vocal: six years or so with collegiate a cappella choirs, a stint with the Navy's Bluejacket Choir, and three years singing bass on a radio gospel quartet. The latter information set him roaring—truly—with laughter and he said, "Now that's the kind of job I'd like to have."

He told me not to worry about the renown of the visiting artists. "You're the kind of critic I like: you write about what you hear. If you have a decent musical ear that's enough. Write about what you hear, not what you thought you were supposed to hear." He said profanely, and he was rather profane, "Nothing irks my butt like some goddam Juilliard graduate, sitting there with a score on his or her lap, circling every goddam semidemihemiquaver we run through." I laughed and said that I was at least qualified enough to know that a semidemi-hemiquaver was a sixty-fourth note. Alvis Earl "Froggie" Rogers, my roommate in college, while a horn player, was also the drum major, and he kept a drumming pad and sticks by his bed, beating out such things as semidemihemiquavers while doing paradiddles and flam paradiddles.

Although Arthur Fiedler was the best known conductor in the U. S. and the Boston Pops was more popular than almost any symphony orchestra, even its Boston Symphony parent, I'm sure he had suffered the slings and arrows of over-qualified critics who sneered at the idea of popularizing classical music—not to mention making classical interpretations of "Hit Parade" tunes. Pardon me for forgetting there are those who don't know that the "Lucky Strike Hit Parade" was a radio program, later on television, which for almost twenty years was a weekly ritual with youngish listeners, featuring the top ten popular songs of the week.

My second year for Fiedler and the Boston Pops to play our town, the Maestro remembered me as "the Hymn Singer," and we had another charming evening in both the concert hall and the living room of the hostess. Fiedler was famous for his love of firefighters and fire-fighting—he was made "Honorary Fire Chief" by several dozen cities—and I told him about observing a genuine Chinese fire drill that proceeded with the chaotic abandon such exercises were alleged to take. He whooped and hollered, shouting the vernacular catch-word regarding such drills.

That night Arthur Fiedler told a joke which I have retold many times—and remember, he could be profane. A big drunken brawler came into a quiet bar and challenged, "I can lick any man in this bar." No one responded and the brawler yelled, "Yer a goddam bunch of cowards." Again, no one responded. The brawler approached a man sitting at the bar having a drink. "You wanna fight?" he asked. The man said, "No," without looking up from his drink. "Why doncha wanna fight?" the brawler asked. "I'm a Quaker. Quakers don't believe in fighting," the man answered. This puzzled the brawler who glowered at the man. "If you're a Quaker, let's hear you talk some Quaker." The man at the bar said quietly, "Fuck thee."

Rise Stevens

A Few Nays Now and Then
Rise Steven's Angry Army

*I*n the years I covered music, the-ater, movies and the arts, I heard very few concerts or saw very few live per-formances of any kind that seemed to show an artist letting down from his or her best. There were a few times when a singer apologized for a cold, a sore throat or sheer weariness, but when that happened the listeners quickly forgave whatever the artist thought might impede the pleasure.

The one concert during which I felt the audience was let down in-volved the beautiful operatic and movie star mezzo-soprano, Rise Stevens. She was near fame's peak and the house had sold out a cou-ple of weeks before she came to Abilene. I had played my 45 rpm set of her *Carmen* so much it was almost playing through to the other side. (Rise Stevens had "created the role" in the glitteringly successful new Metropolitan Opera production.)

But this concert, I wrote, was downright desultory in spots, not of-ten rising to the ardent levels she was famous for achieving. One in-stance of this was with her "Habanera" from *Carmen*. By this time Miss Stevens had sung it so often she could do it in her sleep—and she sang it that way that night. She leaned against the piano, occa-sionally clicking the requisite castanets, seldom displaying any of the passion the song expresses.

I don't know what caused this lassitude. It could have been the comparative remoteness of our town, although concert performers seldom possess much national geography. They know little towns of Italy and Germany better than of the U. S. She could have been weary from a long concert tour, she may have been suffering from a headache, or who knows? I had talked with her briefly that afternoon at her hotel and she seemed a trifle put out with her accompanist—or was it my imagination?

At any rate, when my review came out with its one or two critical comments, a rainstorm of harsh and fervid judgment came down on my head, not from Miss Stevens but from her fan clubs. The general tone was how dare some unknown from Abilene, Texas ("where is that and who are you?") write these things about this sublime singer. I recall the national president of the fan clubs, a woman from New Haven, took particular umbrage, challenging me to come to Connecticut "and say what you did about Rise Stevens." I didn't dare. Besides, Connecticut was way out of our circulation territory.

The Belt: Below and Above

As related before, the amusements editor in Abilene faced a small mountain of a task singlehandedly appraising almost everything or everybody who came to town. I tried to keep a cool soul even when offered that tritest letter of complaint: "I wonder if the music critic

and I attended the same concert, etc." But when I was unfairly confronted by someone who knew better, I could be pretty defensive, even feisty.

At one point I was invited to join several other amusements writers in Dallas for a preview of a new Paramount picture, our reward being a special dinner and reservations at a new Statler-Hilton Hotel. The film being previewed, *The Buccaneer*, with Yul Brynner, turned out to be a Grade B picture with nothing much to recommend it but a Grade A star. When I returned to Abilene I wrote a Sunday column not about *The Buccaneer* but about an old film salesman I had met in

Yul Brunner

Dallas who had traveled West Texas in the early days of movies—back when the screen was a canvas sheet and the projectionist had to let the reels of the film wind off into a peach basket and rewind by hand after each showing. I figured I did Paramount a favor not to dwell overlong on *The Buccaneer*.

Monday morning, after that Sunday column, when I came to work on my desk was a furious telegram from the Paramount flak in Dallas. It wound down with the remark, "After all the money Paramount spent on you, the least you could have done was write about the studio's new picture." I was not pleased with the tone. I wired back, collect "Someday I may whore, but when I do my price will not be a five dollar steak and a night at the Statler-Hilton."

A Fitting Role Doesn't Fit

It always puzzled me how some of the reviews I wrote got back to the performer I wrote about. I will admit, I was now and then guilty of writing cute criticism, little phrases I felt were harmless enough and made good reading. Once I wrote rather slightingly about Kathryn Grant—the former Olive Grandstaff of Austin, Texas, and, at that time, recently wedded second wife of Bing Crosby. She had appeared in some Hollywood pseudo-Arabian Nights epic in which she was portrayed as a maiden menaced by a giant—a depiction that, on the screen, reduced her to about six inches in height. I remarked that at last, there was a role that fitted her talent.

Not long after this the entertainment chairman of the Veterans of Foreign Wars (VFW) chapter in Abilene called me very excited. The VFW was bringing to town Mrs. Bing Crosby! Wasn't that wonderful? And the boys wanted to have me escort her for the afternoon. Well, I was not a member, despite being qualified, but I had dozens of friends who were, and this was the most ambitious undertaking the local chapter had ever undertaken, so I said, sure. I told myself there was only the slightest of chances Kathy Grant Crosby would have seen my review, and even if she had, who cared what some West Texas smart aleck had written?

Well, Mrs. Bing Crosby (Kathryn Grant) arrived and, after a welcoming committee outlined her day, she was introduced to me as part-time driver and escort. When told who (and what) I was she very

Kathryn Grant and Bing Crosby
at the Academy Awards, before their marriage.

pleasantly acknowledged the introduction and I felt relieved. After a rather invigorating lunch—as VFW lunches were in those days, the club being allowed to keep members' liquor—she gave a humorous, Texas-tinged view of Hollywood. Someone asked her what it was like being married to Bing Crosby, the legend. She smiled and rubbed her (shapely) *derrière.* "Bing's idea of a good time," she lamented, "is freezing your butt all day in a duck blind."

In the car, we had a few minutes before her next appointment and she said we might as well just park and wait, that she was exhausted after her celebrations at the VFW Hall.

I was still a bit uncomfortable, but Kathy (which she had insisted everyone call her) had been such a great guest and had showed her native Texas charm so successfully, that I suddenly blurted out, "Kathy . . . I don't imagine you saw it originally, but I made a cheap crack about your acting in a column a few weeks back. But I want to apologize here and now."

She looked at me real hard. "I saw that column within days after you wrote it," she said, "and it made me furious. When I was asked to come to Abilene all I could think of was that I had to meet that," she paused and smiled, "son-of-a-bitch who wrote it. I started to say hell no." She smiled broadly. "I still think you were a mean s.o.b. for saying what you did, but I kinda like you. And besides, there's no use carrying grudges, is there?"

We spent the remainder of her day having a great time.

The Alamo Without Me

John Wayne on the set as Rooster Cogburn, with Glen Campbell (left) and Hal Wallis (right).

On another occasion when one of my columns drew blood it was not the actor's blood: it was mine. After some John Wayne movie or another—I think it was *The Barbarian and the Geisha*—I had given the showing a less than enthusiastic review and criticized The Duke's accent when cast as some totally un-midwest character. I had first encountered John Wayne deep in my childhood when I had seen him in *Telegraph Trails*, a picture I've never heard of again (the old nitrate film may have gone to dust in the can). I didn't just automatically scorn John Wayne movies, the way some critics were doing. In the case of *The Barbarian and the Geisha*, once again I was writing for a limited circulation audience, but I was overheard.

When John Wayne was acting in and directing *The Alamo*, all the film critics across Texas were picked up by special bus and taken to Happy Shahan's Alamo Village near San Antonio, where the movie was being filmed. They spent a day on the set, talking with the actors and being feted in general: All the Texas film writers but one. Me.

I didn't pay much attention to the slight, figuring I might be aghast at what was being done to Texas history if I went. Later I discovered that when the statewide visits were proposed, John Wayne X-ed my name off the list with the remark, "I'm not having that son-of-a-bitch on my set!" When told of this I was puzzled. What did

John Wayne have against me, whom he had never met, writing for a 27,000 circulation newspaper? Then I discovered who and why. Wayne's makeup man, called "Shotgun" Britton, had attended Hardin-Simmons University in Abilene and continued to keep up with local affairs through a subscription to the *Abilene Reporter-News*. He had shown my review to John Wayne.

I never met Shotgun, but he taught me not to go off half-cocked thinking what I wrote wouldn't be seen by the elevated figure in question.

★ ★ ★

There was (almost) a sequel to the John Wayne segment. In the late 1960s, when I was Book Editor of the *Dallas Times Herald*, I found Charles Portis's first book, *Norwood*, so amusing I did a glowing review of it. The publisher sent me the galleys (proofs) on the author's next book, *True Grit*, and quoted my enthusiastic response on the first edition jacket. When I left the *Times Herald* to assume a writing fellowship at the late J. Frank Dobie's country place, Paisano, near Austin, Portis and I became friends by telephone. Portis excitedly called to tell me film rights to *True Grit* had been sold and John Wayne was to play Rooster Cogburn, the male lead. Portis had been given an invitation to visit the set of this Oklahoma picture being shot in Colorado. I thought, hey! maybe I could join Portis and sneak my way onto John Wayne's set. But alas for coincidence—Portis cancelled his trip for the time being and I lost my chance. This turned out to be the best picture John Wayne made. He won an Academy Award for his acting—but there was no happy Hollywood ending to my John Wayne stories.

A Starlit Honeymoon

*T*he *Abilene Reporter-News* had a weekly contest called "News Tips" through which readers could earn as much as five dollars for the best tip of the week, or two dollars and fifty cents for the next best. One night when I was working the City Desk a call came in

Robert Wagner and Natalie Wood

from a very excited man who said, "You're not goin' to believe this, but I just saw an elephant on U. S. Highway 80. This side of Merkel." I took the man's name, in case this turned out *not* to be a pink elephant, and had scarcely cradled the phone when another call came in about an elephant on U. S. 80. Within minutes we had gotten three or four more calls. U. S. 80 was the "Bankhead Highway," the major coast-to-coast highway through the south and southwest so there were lots of travelers. Well, it developed that the elephant was part of a small traveling circus and the owner (who was more shaken than the motorists) told us the poor beast had fallen out of the truck which was carrying it, and been killed by the fall. The Managing Editor, who made the newsroom's monetary decisions, only awarded our first caller two-fifty, which, as the farm editor noted, wasn't exactly an elephantine prize.

But now and then the News Tips feature paid off for the amusements editor. One afternoon as I was mulling over fate or some more serious topic, I got a call from a man who identified himself as a mechanic at Western Chevrolet, a large establishment on west U. S. 80. The mechanic said, "Hey, listen. Natalie Wood and Robert Wagner came in here a few minutes ago. Does that qualify as a News Tip?" I asked if they were still there but he said no, they'd taken the courtesy van into town and the van hadn't come back yet.

"What on earth are they doing in Abilene?" I asked, more or less aloud. I knew that they had just married and were supposed to be honeymooning somewhere in the east—even more reason to ask what they were doing in our town.

"Well, Wagner's got him a new Corvette," my informant informed me, "an' he's got it in for its 5000-mile checkup. It's free on a Corvette, you know."

After I hung up the phone (why do we say, "hung up," when we almost inevitably lay it down?) I asked myself what I would do in a small West Texas town if I were a movie star and I was on my honeymoon with my wife, who was also a movie star, and my new Corvette's odometer rolled over 5000 miles and I had taken it in for its 5000-mile (free) checkup, which would take a couple or so hours? The answer wasn't as complicated as the question: we would go to the movies.

I called the Paramount, the beautiful first-run house, and asked the doorman if Natalie Wood and Robert Wagner had been in? He let out a whoop and yelled, "I told you!" at someone and then said to me, yes, they'd come in but the rest of the crew just couldn't believe it was them. They'd bought popcorn, too.

I went to the Paramount and an usher whispered they were midway on a rear row. The picture was *Rally 'Round the Flag*. I slipped into the row and, in the dark introduced myself and said I didn't want to disturb them, just wanted to be sure it was who it was. Natalie Wood said, "Have you seen the picture?" I said I hadn't, and she said, "Here, sit between us and share our popcorn." I didn't want to sit between the honeymooners, but the invitation to join them seemed sincere, so I did. After the movie Robert Wagner called for the Western Chevrolet van, and I apologized that my wife had kept our car or I'd take them back to the Chevrolet place.

After we left the Paramount to go to the corner drugstore for a Coke, a good many people did a double-take at this pretty girl and this handsome man with their familiar faces, and you could see these citizens thinking, "No . . . it can't be."

The van was driven by a big, good natured black man who laughed and said, "I'm carryin' some pretty famous folks, ain't I?"

Natalie said, "Yes indeed. This is Mr. Greene, amusements editor of the *News and Reporter*." I forgave her mistake, but felt a delicious shiver of conspiracy go down my spine: Natalie Wood had recommended me.

This was the first marriage for both Natalie and Robert. They would divorce and marry others, but would then marry again, and they were full of little things like hand holding. Natalie Wood was a small woman but with a beauty that went beyond sexiness—although there was plenty of that. She had been in movies since age four and had just finished playing the title role in *Marjorie Morningstar*. She was explaining to me that her breasts were too small for the low cut dress she wore in a dancing scene—Robert protesting, "Now honey, that's not true"—and how she had been taped so tight, "I was positively bosomy." But believe it or not, what we really spent most of our conversation on was books, starting with the Herman Wouk novel she had just filmed. The book, about a young woman having to face decisions internal and external she didn't want to have to make, reminded her of herself, Natalie said. Both the honeymooners were readers and both were eager to talk about the current literary scene.

We seemed to get along so famously that I suggested they come to the Greenes' apartment for supper. I assured them that my wife Betty was a good cook, a book reader, and a frequent moviegoer who liked both of them—all of which was true. After supper they could pick up the 5000-mile Corvette and continue westward.

Natalie said she was afraid my wife wouldn't appreciate us "moving in on her this way," but I assured her there would be no problem and that I wanted my wife to meet them as friends, not just as celebrities. I almost had them persuaded. Western Chevrolet would, I knew, arrange something suitable with their car; probably deliver it to where we lived just a few blocks south of the dealership—any number of volunteers would drive it to get a look at Natalie. But, after some hesitation, the Wagners decided they must hurry on. One or both had a new picture to start sometime within a matter of days. "We really would like to stay but we have to get as far as we can tonight," Robert said, and a new Corvette with only 5,000 miles on it might get you a good long ways at night on a West Texas highway.

So they got in their Corvette and roared on toward Hollywood. Natalie kissed me on the cheek as we said goodbye. My wife was very disappointed they hadn't stayed for supper. I never told her that that night I didn't wash my face where Natalie Wood kissed me.

A Rowdy Children's Concert

*A*lthough the Army closed Camp Barkeley in 1945, Dyess Air Force Base, a large B-52 bomber base, had opened in 1955 and provided Abilene with an additional audience for cultural affairs. Abilene was also fortunate that any number of military personnel who had been stationed at Camp Barkeley came back to the growing little city to live. One of these imports was Robert Tiffany, a serious music student who played the trumpet professionally—in fact, had led a top-notch dance band while he was at Camp Barkeley. After the war, he and his wife, Clarine, a lovely local lady who was also a highly trained musician, were active in all the musical events the town proposed, though Bob eventually put away his golden trumpet.

Bob and Clarine visited the New York music scene at least twice a year and on one trip they had heard Leonard Warren, a popular Metropolitan Opera tenor and on returning to Abilene they decided that if possible Leonard Warren would sing for the Civic Music Association, of which Bob was president. One of the things they had liked was Warren's affability. There was none of the halo of arrogance that so often accompanied high level artists.

Leonard Warren

The Leonard Warren concert in Abilene, well advertised, drew a full house, and Bob Tiffany introduced him almost as a personal friend. The singer was greeted with a generous round of applause when he strode on stage. His first number was a bravura piece that displayed his technique and it, too, was given suitable appreciation. But somewhere in his second or third song, one that involved a good bit of *fortissimo* then *pianissimo*, as Leonard Warren was expressively offering a quietly dramatic passage, a voice suddenly spoke out over the hushed air calling: "Louder."

It was said in a toneless monotone, not so much a command as a suggestion. Warren, missing only the slightest beat (his eyes darted just a fraction of an instant) increased his tone, but, through mastery of his art, did so without destroying the tension of the soft passage. As he moved into a further passage, increasing the *fortissimo* slightly but skillfully, that toneless voice was heard again: "Louder."

Leonard Warren continued to sing maybe a dozen notes, then stopped and gazed fearfully, not just across the audience but around the stage, trying to find, perhaps, if the hollow voice was coming from the wings. A look of despair flushed his face and looking down at the front row he screamed, "Get these children out of here . . . they're making so much noise I can't be heard. I won't go on with the concert. Get 'em out of here!" With that he marched off stage, along with his baffled accompanist.

It became Bob Tiffany's task, as President of Abilene Civic Music, to come on stage and announce, "Will the mothers of these children please come get them?" He paused, looking helplessly at the innocent music lovers sitting below him. "Can you come quickly so we may go on with the concert?"

Several of the mothers, and one father, came down to the front, some obviously not sure if their child was among the guilty. The father looked up at Bob and demanded, "Where th' hell are we supposed to put 'em?" The audience laughed, and several people cheered. When Bob replied, "I guess they can sit on your lap," the audience howled and someone shouted that the children ought to be seated on stage.

What Leonard Warren didn't know—neither did most of his listeners—was that a fine old lawyer named J. McAlister Stevenson was in the audience, as he was for most cultural events. He was a generous supporter of the arts, but had a major disability: a hearing deficiency he wouldn't acknowledge. He was not just hard of hearing, he was on a downhill slope toward deafness. Like so many nearly deaf people, he didn't realize how acute his hearing loss had become.

I am convinced that when he said, "Louder" he was actually thinking to himself. He didn't realize his thought was translated into audible speech. His second call of "Louder" was merely a further reflection on the faintness, to him, of the proceedings. I'm sure he was mildly puzzled at all the hullabaloo on stage, but didn't comprehend he had caused it.

I believe it was Clarine Tiffany who first grasped what had happened. She went backstage and explained, with apologies, to Leonard Warren, convincing him that the old lawyer had not tried to turn up the singer's volume but had been speaking to himself.

Leonard Warren, by now accusing himself of over-reacting, seized on the idea. Clarine and Bob both assured him that the crowd was on his side, that they had been as outraged as he was at that call of "Louder." And I, who for once was not backstage, would have agreed.

The singer made the humblest apology one can imagine. "I've never done anything like this before," he said, "and I have no excuse." He looked around, "And I wouldn't blame you if everyone had walked out on me. I deserved it." There were voices denying this, but along with some of the mothers, a number of persons had left the auditorium. Mr. Warren offered to refund, personally, the ticket cost to anyone who felt wronged.

"And please . . . let the children return to these seats," he swept his hand toward the front row chairs, "I will sing a special number for these children." No one, as I recall, wanted his money back and the program continued with the kind of zealous enthusiasm aroused by such an unlooked for occurrence. Leonard Warren sang not just one but a suite of children's songs. He sang several encores and even offered to return and do a free concert for Abilene. For those who were there, it turned out to be one of the most successful concerts in the city's history—and I don't believe J. McAlister Stevenson realized what a debt we owed him.

A Rookie at Bat

There was a time in Mid-America when every small town boy wanted to be a sports writer. There were good reasons for this; the sports writer was a local hero, and in most small towns, sports was the main topic of conversation and the main source of local news. Within the newspaper, the sports editor was better paid than the other departmental editors, and generally had more clout. If the sports staff lost a member at a critical time—such as the start of the high school football season—the sports editor could pick just about anyone he wanted off the news staff. That had been the way I was inducted into sports writing at the *Abilene Reporter-News*.

As an Abilene sports writer I covered everything from university to small town high school sports. Small town football rivalry in Texas is more than fierce; it is vehement. In West Texas the entire town will close down early on game day, sometimes close for the day, then drive astonishing distances to the foe's city for the 7 P.M. game. (In a few rivalries the visitors bring their own food and drink so as not to have to spend "one goddam nickel" in the opposing town.)

Covering this kind of football could be rough, even hazardous. I spent more than one country game in (or on—there was no shelter) a "press box" which consisted of three 1 x 8 boards nailed together, situated twenty feet up on one of the light poles, and reached by ladder. I usually shared that "press box" with a local announcer, most often the Baptist preacher—the Baptist church was the biggest business in some West Texas towns, and sometimes the church owned the public address system. Sooner or later, the preacher would lose his objectivity and begin yelling, "We made it!" or, "Catch him . . . catch him!"

I got chased out of town, via auto, after one game where the opposing crowd thought I was the one doing the biased commentary from up on the pole. Lucky for me, this group went after the wrong car, not dreaming that a big-town (pop. 47,000) sports writer (fifty-five dollars per week) might be driving a ten-year-old Hudson. After another game—an annual grudge match—I was mistaken for the local radio announcer and a big disgruntled lout (fueled by something stronger than Dr Pepper) came racing up the wooden stands yelling what he intended to do to me. He gave a lunge in my direction—I was at another one of those open press boxes—and, retreating backward, I stuck out my clip board. It was a defensive gesture, but it caught him square on the Adam's apple! The last I saw of him as I ran down to my getaway car, he was standing, gulping for air, having lost all inclination to whip the skinny posterior of me or anybody else.

At the *Reporter-News* I was working under a sports editor who supplemented his income in two ways: by being Official Scorer for the Abilene Blue Sox baseball team in the West Texas-New Mexico League—the accepted way the league paid off the sports editors—and (under the table) by seeing to it that the weekly wrestling news got decent play on the sports pages.

One night after I'd been a sports writer for nearly a year, this Official Scorer came in late from a Blue Sox game and threatened to fire me when he discovered I had forgotten to print wrestling promoter Benny Wilson's weekly grunt-and-groan submission.

I had pretty much been running the sports department for the sports editor that summer (at no increase in salary), and this petty accusation enraged me. I charged over to his desk and demanded he stand up so I could whip him. Fortunately for me, and perhaps him, he was too drunk to do either, and we had no further open conflicts.

In defense of promoter Benny Wilson (though not of his payoff), he was a fascinating character whose own adventures as a wrestler in Mexico, Central America and the southern U. S. were superior to anything he offered on the weekly card—even Gorgeous George and Lou Thiez, the "legitimate" World Heavyweight Champion at that time. Benny's torso had multiple cigarette and cigar burns where overly passionate fans had reached through the ropes to get to him if he appeared to be winning over the hometown favorite. In the match that ended Benny's active career, his opponent, who was scheduled to lose, cheated, and broke Benny's back.

When I first got into newspapering, I hadn't thought about becoming a sports writer—and although my first couple of years as one were enjoyable, I could see my sports writing career heading toward boredom. I could cover football, but the sports editor would always take over the biggest games. I didn't know (or like) basketball that well—this was before black players redefined the game—and baseball was handled by the Official Scorer. So, in self-defense, I became the track and field expert.

I grew to love the thinly clads, as the runners used to be called, and when I read myself being quoted in national track publications, it helped my ego, if not my salary. But my job was made easy because just as I became the staff track writer, Abilene Christian College made Oliver Jackson track coach. From the beginning Coach Jackson showed himself to be one of the great ones, as was proved by the national records his relay teams set, and such U. S. Olympians he produced as sprinter Bobby Morrow, winner of three Olympic gold medals, sprinter Bill Woodhouse, and field man Earl Young.

The Texas Relays, at the University of Texas at Austin, is the first big national outdoor track and field meet. Back in the 1950s, some major league baseball club would be stopping in Austin at the same time to play an exhibition game with the University of Texas baseball team. At the 1950 Texas Relays, the first morning, as Coach Jackson and I were sitting down to breakfast, who should walk in the hotel dining room but the entire New York Yankee baseball team. The coaches and the big city sports writers immediately took over the stars, such as Joe DiMaggio, Phil Rizzuto or Chief Allie Reynolds.

I found myself at a table with a couple of Yankee rookies, one of whom told me he came from Commerce, Oklahoma. He was tickled when I said I knew where it was. I'd attended Kansas State Teachers Collage at Pittsburg and was acquainted with that coal and lead mining corner where Oklahoma, Kansas and Missouri come together.

His name was Mickey Mantle and he said he'd always wanted to play for the Yankees, even though everybody in his part of the world was for the St. Louis Cardinals. He'd signed with the Yankees in 1949 at age eighteen but this was going to be his first year in the majors. I said I'd read about him when he signed—terrific hitter. He told me how his dad had put a baseball in his cradle for him to "wean" on. He seemed confident that he could crack the Yankee lineup. I couldn't help but notice he kept glancing over at the big shot tables where the fabled heroes were eating. Somehow, he seemed to know he was bound to get there.

We had a pleasant breakfast and when we all shook hands he even thanked me for sharing the meal. (I did pick up the check.) I told Oliver Jackson the boy struck me as having star potential. Oliver said he'd heard the rookie couldn't run the bases. "Maybe he'll just hit home runs," I laughed, unconsciously prophetic.

I never met Mickey Mantle again, even though I lived in Dallas during the later years when he did. Only a sad footnote to our chance encounter: in 1995 when he underwent a liver transplant, a reporter called to ask what advice, as a heart transplant, I would give The Mick. I offered a couple of suggestions, but Mickey Mantle died before he could use anyone's transplant advice.

It Happened One Night

The midwest had a successful basketball tournament named the National Association of Intercollegiate Basketball (NAIB). It involved some hot hoop schools that didn't play in a conference and for years, reaching the NAIB finals was the equivalent of being one of "The Final Four" today. But by 1950, more and more larger schools were in the National Collegiate Athletics Association (NCAA) and the NCAA refused to let schools be members unless they participated in all sports, which would have been suicide for some of the schools that had great basketball and track teams but couldn't field a football team.

Several schools met in Emporia, Kansas, and decided to have a NAIB track and field meet. Some of the school officials and coaches went further and asked why not form the NAIA—change the National Association of Intercollegiate Basketball into the National Association of Intercollegiate Athletics? With some trepidation this was finally agreed on. I was able to get McMurry College of Abilene, for the price of a new "Red Dog" cinder track, to host the first track and field meet, using empty dorms and cafeteria facilities to house and feed the athletes.

One of the stipulations was that there must be no discrimination shown toward the black athletes, Texas still being in the clutches of

Dick Gregory

segregation. Many of the NAIA schools had black athletes and this point had been muchly debated when the Texas location was offered. McMurry College and the city of Abilene held to this pledge. All the runners, the jumpers, sprinters, hurdlers, the discus hurlers and javelin throwers, the shot-putters—everyone—lived together and ate together and competed together without a visible wrinkle, so far as meet officials knew.

The night of the finals I was down on the sideline watching the competition, keeping times and distances on a clipboard. A black athlete wearing the uniform of the Southern Illinois Salukis and I got into conversation and we talked about the meet and how it had been put together and whether it was working, in racial terms. The Illinois miler said he was surprised, frankly, but pleased that this sort of thing could take place in the deep south (his term). I said Abilene was different, being a new West Texas town, never having had a plantation economy or slavery. We had a mutually stimulating conversation (stimulating to me, at least) about racial discrimination. I didn't try to defend discrimination in Texas or the South, but I didn't want this visitor thinking I was the redneck some people thought all Texans must be. I told him my mother and my grandmother, with whom I grew up, had forbidden me to use the word "nigger." He looked at me with an eyebrow raised grinned, "And so you never have?"

His event was called, we shook hands, and it was several years later I realized that Dick Gregory, the actor, comedian, writer, and activist, was the same Dick Gregory as the miler who had been a Southern Illinois Saluki that night in Abilene, Texas, at the first NAIA track meet.

Chance Encounters
in the 1960s

Artie Shaw with his collection of chess sets.

A.C. signing his fiction,
The Highland Park Woman,
at a Dallas book store.

My Unrecorded Newsroom Duet

$\mathscr{I}$got a job at the *Dallas Times Herald* in 1960 after I had re-signed, retroactively, from the *Abilene Reporter-News*. The Managing Editor of the *Reporter-News* had come over to my desk and reported that the publisher insisted I was not writing enough afternoon features. I tried to point out that I had something or other in the paper every day and edited a double-truck (two page) Amusements opening on Sundays. I had written a complicated feature story that just the day before had run "above the banner," the place of honor for a newspaper story, but apparently it was to be quantity, not quality. I could see that my hometown journalism career was over, so I said, "Okay, I quit." The M.E. asked, "When? In three weeks? A month?"

"No," I replied, haughtily, "I quit retroactively twenty minutes ago." And I hit the road looking for a job. (Actually, the M.E. was not a bad guy but, as is, or was, the case with so many Managing Editors, he was cowed by the publisher.)

I finally went to work for the *Dallas Times Herald*, but only after I had waited three weeks to go on the payroll. I had gotten a bad recommendation from the *Reporter-News*. I went to work on the rewrite desk. On an afternoon paper the reporters on the various beats, such as city hall, the police department ("The Cop Shop"), county offices, or the federal beat, do not have time to come in and write their stories. They telephone the rewrite desk and the rewrite man does the writing. The rewrite man's name never appeared on the stories, although we on the rewrite desk did prizewinning pieces—for the beat men.

The newsroom, where the rewrite desk was located, and where news editors and reporters worked, used to attract many strange, lonely, or sensational people. One day I returned from my thirty-minute lunch break to find Shirley Maclaine, the film star, seated at my rewrite slot, doodling Japanese characters on a piece of copy paper. (A segment of TV's *Route 66* was being filmed in our newsroom.) Another time we were suddenly thrown into an uproar by a brace of huge ravens swooping and darting about the big room in celebration of Alfred Hitchcock's new movie, *The Birds*.

On a day when I took the noon watch, there were just a handful of us in the newsroom around the City Desk. I saw a nondescript man come wandering in from the elevator. He looked around, obviously not knowing just where he was. I went over to him and asked if I could help him or who it was he wanted to see. He looked around, as if he sought a friendly face, and asked me, "Is this where the entertainment department is?" I said yes, but I said I didn't see anyone there right now. "Probably out having a free lunch off somebody," I laughed. The man laughed too and said, "I'll bet that's right."

He said he just wanted to let the entertainment people know he was in town, playing a certain club for a few days. "I don't know if they might want to come down and hear us, maybe," he said, then made an attempt to joke. "We may not be as popular as we were a few years back." This was an old story to me, the former critic, having heard it from everybody from Broadway players to Grade B film stars.

"I'll give Don a note," I said, referring to the young night club writer, "and what's your name?"

"M'name's Al Dexter," he said, and hesitated. I knew he was about to explain to me who he was, or had been. And on that instant I was inspired to start singing, "'Now there was ol' Al Dexter, he always had his fun . . . .'" It was a line from his famous World War II hit, "Pistol Packin' Mama."

Al Dexter's face brightened, he finished the line himself, then motioned I should join him in the chorus, and I did:

"Lay that pistol down, babe, lay that pistol down,
Pistol packin' mama, lay that pistol down."

By the time we finished, the ten or so people in the newsroom had gathered around us. They demanded another verse, which Al Dexter and I did, with the crowd joining in, clapping in rhythm on the familiar chorus.

So, that night did I go out to the night club, get called up to the stand, and after he had told the crowd our story, joined Al Dexter in our vocal routine? No, I'm afraid that's not the way the story ended. Before I went off work, I left Al Dexter's note about his presence in town at the Entertainment Desk, and heard no more of Al Dexter or his Dallas gig. That newsroom duet was the beginning and the end of my life as a country and western singer.

The Cotton Bowl Governor or a Tux for Danny

In the first couple of years after I began working there, I became a sort of utility outfielder of criticism and coverage at the *Times Herald*. My services were even called on by our famous sports editor, William Forrest (Blackie) Sherrod. He asked me to do sideline and dressing room color at a Cotton Bowl game where the University of Mississippi ("Old Miss") and the University of Texas were to play. It was on this assignment I learned one of the secrets of being a public figure.

Among the attractions of being part of the press coverage of the Cotton Bowl was a black-tie party on the night before the game, sponsored by the Cotton Bowl Association. The press was only a minor part of this show. Financial and political bigwigs outnumbered the Fourth Estate. This party was where, as West Texas says it, "they put th' big pot in th' little 'un."

Dan Jenkins, of the *Times Herald* sports staff—who became a *Sports Illustrated* staffer, a successful novelist, *Semi-Tough*, and screen writer—warned me of the prestigious nature of the event and asked me if I had a tuxedo. I told him I supposed I would rent one.

Ross Barnett on the sidelines.

He said that in the first place with Cotton Bowl parties and New Year's Eve parties taking place throughout Dallas, I'd never find one for rent, and in the second place, if I expected to stay in newspapering "and be any sort of a public figure," I should have my own tuxedo. It was hick-town to rent one.

I told myself, "Surely you want to be a public figure," and besides, Dan was from Fort Worth, so I recognized his native social superiority over someone from Abilene. At any rate, I hastily bought a tuxedo and, with the Cotton Bowl gala as my excuse, talked the store into doing the alterations the same day. The party (lavish), the tux (shawl collar), and my wife (pretty) were great successes—so great my wife had to drive us home at 2 A.M.

At the Cotton Bowl game I shared my stretch of sideline with a suspicious Mississippi state highway patrolman who had been assigned to guard the visiting Governor Ross Barnett. I'm not sure why the patrolman put me under the shadow of doubt; maybe it was because I was a reporter, not a sports writer. I can't think of any other reason—I certainly didn't have a "Yankee" accent, which was (figuratively) the kiss of death. This was the time of "sit-ins" and of "freedom riders," with "foreign" press reports favorable toward the civil rights activists. Newspaper reporters, other than sports writers, were viewed with mistrust throughout the Deep South, especially in Mississippi. It was evident I was not a sports writer or, on this damp and wintery day, I would be up in the fancy (hot free meals) press box.

When Governor Barnett came up to me and introduced himself and we shook hands (under the keen eye of my Mississippi patrolman guard), I was careful not to make any kind of playful motion, like slapping the governor on the back or nudging him in the ribs. After this endorsement by the governor, the Mississippi patrolman and I got along nicely, even when Texas won over Old Miss 12–7.

Governor Barnett later that year would attempt (unsuccessfully) to use the now-forgotten doctrine of "interposition" to try and block the entrance of James Meredith to the University of Mississippi.

But on the occasion of Old Miss in the Cotton Bowl there was no public talk of the racial problems that were spreading over the South—and the entire nation. Neither team had a black player, which tells you how incredibly long ago, by social and cultural timing, that was. I remember clearly standing there on the sideline, watching the two football teams engaged in bowl battle. I thought of all the Texas-born black players who had had to go north to places like Michigan or west to California to play, and what it was costing Texas football teams in national prestige. I knew that with the power football held over Texas, it couldn't last—and it didn't.

Dan Jenkins was right and wrong; a tuxedo proved to be a sound investment. I wore that pre-Cotton Bowl tux for thirty years before I had to buy a new one. But he was wrong about my becoming a public figure because of it. In the television coverage of the Cotton Bowl game one of the cameras picked up Governor Barnett just as he was shaking hands with me. I learned the announcers said "Governor Barnett seems to be shaking hands with some public figure." And I wasn't wearing my tuxedo. So there!

Stanley in Dallasville

*I*n the spring of 1960 I was recently appointed Book Editor of the *Dallas Times Herald*. Almost immediately after that designation I began to be invited to parties and gatherings that included book lovers, authors, and others generally held to be the intellectual cream of Texas society, Dallas branch. Having come from another newspaper where the Book Editor ranked just above the Religious Editor and far below the Farm Editor, I was unprepared for the social acceptance Dallas gave a totally unknown newcomer. Wait—I was not totally unknown. The first fancy book party where I was a guest was in the elaborate Highland Park home of John William Rogers, an author, playwright, and former Book Editor of the *Times Herald.* Several years before John William had written *The Lusty Texans of Dallas*, a kind of social history of the city. I had been given the book to review and while enjoying the writing—Rogers wrote well about Dallas society of which he was a stalwart part—I decried what I perceived was a worshipful attitude toward wealth on the part of the author. I think I even used the phrases "kow-towing" and "bowing to the rich." Two weeks later, in his Sunday book column, John William Rogers blasted this unknown critic (question mark) from where—Abilene, Texas? Thus, you must believe me, I dreaded meeting John William Rogers, even though many years had passed since my review.

I was enjoying the affair at the Rogerses, looking out a set of French windows down a long, softly lighted sward to a leaping fountain at the end of the garden aisle. John William and his wife, herself a charming writer named Kenneth Horan, had seen to it that I was comfortable. I thanked God I appeared to be forgiven. As I stood contemplating the sight, John William came to my side and told how he had planned and installed the lovely scene before me. As he talked I felt a pang of guilt, remembering the review I had given his book.

After a few more observations about the garden, he asked me how the literary world looked to me. I mentioned two or three Texas books that were on the way, then decided I would feel awkward every time I met either of the Rogerses if I didn't clear the air—and take the consequences. In a rush of words I admitted I had given his book a harsh review. "Youthful prejudice may have taken over my critical apparatus," I paused, "and it irritated the hell out of you. And I don't blame you."

John William said, "A. C., I've never forgotten that review. It was the worst review my book got . . . but I shouldn't have responded the way I did. It was childish of me." He paused again, "I hated you for it. In fact, making up the guest list for tonight, I asked Kenneth, 'Are we

Stanley Marcus

obliged to invite that guy?' She said yes, that we had both been book critics and we'd trampled on a lot of feelings ourselves."

He extended his hand, saying, "So if you'll forgive my outraged response, I'll forgive your harsh review." I reached out my hand and shook his, and as we did I saw from the corner of my eye a man with a camera squatting down, taking a picture of our reconciliation. John William turned and said, "Mr. Greene, our cameraman is that noted photographer, Stanley Marcus." I shook the hand of Mr. Marcus, wishing my wife, who hadn't moved the children to Dallas yet, could be there. I remarked on his camera, a less than pocket-sized Minox. "Yes, we are now carrying the Minox in our photography department of Neiman-Marcus," he said. "The company sent me one to try out." John William said to me, "It's dangerous to be around Stanley, nowadays. He'll stick that thing in your face and shoot you before you can defend yourself."

About then someone called the host away and I started to explain who I was but Stanley said, "I know who you are. I read the book pages carefully." He told me that when he was graduating from Harvard if he could have chosen his future he would have wanted to open a book and fine art store in southern France. As we parted Stanley said he would send me prints from the film he had shot.

Shortly after the Rogers party Stanley Marcus invited me to have lunch at the Zodiac Room with him and Mr. and Mrs. Laurent de Brunhoff, the son and daughter-in-law of the late Jean de Brunhoff. They had taken over the *Babar the Elephant* series which the father had started before World War II.

Stanley Marcus continued to invite me to meet various visiting authors not only at the store but at his home, and we became friends on more than just a book basis. At one such gathering to honor the late

Bennett Cerf, Lon Tinkle, *The Dallas Morning News'* masterful book critic, and I, got Cerf off into what Stanley called his "fertility room" (a display of African and South American pieces) and as if to test the nickname, talked Cerf into a book contract.

I came to know Stanley's late wife, Billie, quite well—in fact, on one occasion when Stanley was out of town, Billie asked me and my wife Betty to help host the visiting Irish writer Seán O'Faoláin. All three of us hurriedly read separately on the Irishman's short stories, then pooled our knowledge. The Marcus children—Jerrie, Wendy and Richard—along with their families, are now longtime friends. I'm godfather to Stanley's granddaughter, Allison Smith.

Stanley married Linda Robinson after Billie's death. In my days as book editor, Linda had been my contact person at the Dallas Public Library when I wanted book and literary news from the system.

In 1984 Stanley published my story, "A Christmas Tree," in a 2 x 3 inch edition from his famous Somesuch Press—the name a play on Nonesuch Road, the East Dallas street Stanley created and named when he built a home there. (In 1996 he published a miniature edition of my China Marine story, "Brandy Miracle.")

From 1975 through 1999, each December Stanley gave his "Good Guys" luncheon for thirty or so male friends, and year to year it included some of the most interesting citizens of our nation. I was named historian of the Good Guys, probably as much for my ability to recite bawdy limericks as for my status as a historian.

Stanley Marcus died January 22, 2002, a few weeks before his ninety-seventh birthday. His funeral was held in the beautiful Morton Meyerson Symphony Hall in downtown Dallas, the only public space sufficient, and appropriate enough, to hold his family, friends and admirers—mourners was not the word for the occasion. Some of us, rather old ourselves, didn't think Stanley would ever die.

And I never got prints of those photos Stanley shot at John William Rogers's home that night in 1960.

Joan Didion and Hermes Nye.
A "chance encounter" that
didn't happen.

A Potpourri of Brief Encounters

Joan Didion and the Little Man Who Wasn't There

*O*nce a young woman named Joan Didion called me, in my position as book editor of the *Dallas Times Herald*, and said she was working on a magazine story about women who moved from the smaller towns into big cities and she thought I might be able to point her toward some Dallas interviews. I said I would do that, and take her to a place where a number of women she seemed to have in mind ate lunch. (I knew her writing, but this was before her film script career began.)

When Ms Didion arrived, I escorted her to the Baker Hotel (since imploded) with the intention of eating at The Baker's Dozen, a nice soup-salad-and-sandwich kind of eatery. But when we got there the line waiting to get in was out the door into the hall. The waiting appeared long, so I suggested we eat at another suitable place, and Ms Didion agreed. She was very polite and self-contained and I hadn't been able to get a real conversation going with her, just "How do you like Dallas?" "Never been here before, but it seems like a pleasant place"—that sort of thing.

The Baker Hotel had a long, rather narrow entry hall that extended from its Commerce Street side all the way to the lobby. Other then The Baker's Dozen and a couple of hotel administrative offices, there were no shops or boutiques located along this entryway. As Ms Didion and I were walking down the hallway toward the exit, a man neared us and I, thinking he was Hermes Nye, a lawyer friend and Dallas folksinger, spoke to him loud and cheerfully: "Hello, Hermes."

The man, obviously a visitor, and even more obviously, one of those taut, nervously alert men, stopped, looked around frantically, then demanded, "Were you speaking to me?" It was an embarrassing mistake, but to cover my confusion I took a bold route. Looking him in the eye I said, "Why no, I was speaking to Hermes Nye." The man again looked frantically for some entity that could be Hermes Nye. There was no one else in the hallway. As Ms Didion and I walked away, she peered cautiously back at the man then at me. The nervous man was still looking, as she and I reached the Commerce Street door.

We walked the two blocks or so to the next restaurant without comment other than her observation that Dallas pedestrians were very polite, waiting patiently for the lights to change when there were no cars approaching. I told her about the time Edna Ferber had been arrested for jaywalking in Dallas and how outraged she was because she had always jaywalked in New York. Ms Didion said that sounded like Edna Ferber.

Just before we entered this second restaurant, she stopped me. "I've been thinking about this all the way here—may I ask, is there such a person or thing as Hermes Nye?"

"Of course there is," I said pleasantly. "But," added sincerely, "it wasn't that fellow at the Baker Hotel." We had a pleasant lunch, and Hermes Nye was not mentioned again.

Not at Home on the Range

On publication day for his book *Midnight Cowboy*, James L. Herlihy, the author, was in Dallas to begin a book-signing tour, as the book opens in West Texas. The young protagonist gets his ideas of life from a West Texas movie drive-in and catches a Greyhound in Big Spring.

Jon Voight (left) and Dustin Hoffman (right) in a scene from Midnight Cowboy. *The author says "Thanks, but I'll pass."*

I asked Herlihy if he was from somewhere in that vast stretch of territory. He said he just rode through on a bus. I took him to lunch at The Cattleman, a fancy steak house in downtown Dallas, which I thought was a suitable place to honor a book and its author on pub day. We had champagne cocktails (you couldn't buy mixed drinks in Texas at the time) and clicked our glasses in salute to *Midnight Cowboy*. He had also written *Blue Denim* and seen it made into a successful movie, but he didn't think *Midnight Cowboy* would have that good a career, he said.

The Cattleman offered a list of free appetizers which included a rib, some kind of barbecued meat, and an item listed as "calf fries." Herlihy and I opted for the latter, and when our appetizers arrived he cut a slice off his calf fry, took a bite and exclaimed, "Tasty!" I realized he didn't know what calf fries—called "prairie oysters" or "Rocky Mountain oysters" depending on where you are eating them—were, but as he found them tasty (and the Cattleman prepared them to perfection), I thought I should tell him. Trying to avoid the vernacular, I used the anatomical description: calf testes.

He looked at his appetizer plate for a moment, then pushed it aside, saying quietly, "Tasty . . . but too rich."

Peppering Things Up

Southern Methodist University English professor Marshall Terry is a novelist whose book, *Tom Northway*, is an American classic by almost

John Updike

any definition. Marsh is also one of those men of infinite jest. One summer a fellow member of the English faculty, spending the season in Europe, asked Professor Terry to look after his closed-up house while he was gone. Terry dutifully went by, twice a week, to check up on things. But one night after 10 P.M. a neighboring woman called him excitedly that she had seen someone trying to break into the absent professor's home. Marsh quickly pulled on his clothes and drove to the site. Just as he arrived a police cruiser pulled up and a uniformed policeman jumped out and hurried toward him.

"I'm Marshall Terry," Marsh said, extending a hand. The policeman shook the hand and exclaimed, "Good to meet you, Marshal. You take the side yard and I'll take the back!"

★ ★ ★

For several years Southern Methodist University literature students annually produced a series of lectures and readings by national writers and poets. Marsh Terry, the faculty organizer of this highly successful program, undertakes to entertain or celebrate the writers. Once, a few years back, John Updike was a guest and Marsh asked me if I would chauffeur him, and the novelist and his wife on a short tour of Dallas, that his venerable sedan was having a bad week. I was happy to comply. We arrived at the Updikes' hotel at mid-morning, and when John Updike and his new second wife, Martha, came down, escorted by Marsh, it seemed to me the two visitors were weary, and I wondered to myself if they might not have preferred to remain in until the time of Updike's talk. But they were gracious and were still at the handholding stage, John deferring to Martha at any question. I asked them if they had any local sights they wanted especially to see, but I could tell Dallas was fairly strange country to them. Marsh suggested the Kennedy assassination site and the guests agreed, and I suggested Southfork Ranch—the TV drama *Dallas* then going strong—and they also agreed.

As we walked to the parked car, John Updike looked east across some low-lying buildings to a tall tower with a clock face that read, ten, two and four.

John stopped, looked at the tower and asked, "What is that?"

"That's a Dallas landmark," I explained. "That's the international headquarters for Dr Pepper."

"That building?" he asked.

"That's right. The clock reads 'Ten, Two and Four' which is a slogan for Dr Pepper."

He said to Martha, "Look, sweetheart . . . right here in Dallas. The world headquarters for Dr Pepper."

And with that they both began to skip along and sing, "I'm a Pepper . . . you're a Pepper . . . we're all Peppers!" It was the television kiddie jingle that had introduced Dr Pepper, an old Texas soft drink, to the northern portion of the nation. John and Martha Updike were elated. The tour of Dallas went unusually well and they were still holding hands and singing, "I'm a Pepper, you're a Pepper!" when they were returned to the hotel.

The Case of a Phantom Keyboard

I covered a few concerts in Dallas, after I joined the *Dallas Times Herald* staff. I was not a member of the arts and entertainment department but now and then there was too much going on in one

John Rosenfield

evening for the staff to stretch across and I was drafted. In fact, when the veteran arts editor was told he was terminally ill, he suggested I be readied as his replacement. But I wouldn't dare step into that mare's nest, trying to direct the work of people who would resent anyone appointed outside their ranks.

One Dallas concert I covered resulted in an amusing contretemps (a word I have never before used) for the competition, *The Dallas Morning News*. The occasion was an appearance by Chilean pianist Claudio Arrau. The critic for the *Morning News* was the famous, authoritative, and crotchety, John Rosenfield. Although we later became friends, at this time he didn't know me. If he looked around the concert hall, he must have thought the *Times Herald* hadn't sent anyone to cover Claudio Arrau's playing.

The first half of the program was unusually long and at the intermission I saw Rosenfield leave his seat and exit the auditorium. I thought he was merely going to get a refreshment or some fresh air but when the concert resumed his seat was still empty. Maybe he was observing a tight A.M. deadline, or maybe he had heard Arrau before and felt he knew what the sounds of the remaining portion would be. The second half of a pianist's concert usually features a composition he is renowned for recording or the work of some composer in whose work he specializes.

What John Rosenfield had not counted on from Claudio Arrau was a sudden change in the program, announced from the stage (with apologies) by the pianist himself. Thus, the later portion of the concert was quite different from what was on the printed program.

But Rosenfield's review next morning in the *Dallas News* was full of praise for Arrau's handling of "the very difficult" work—the work he had not played. My review in the afternoon *Times Herald* made a slightly amused comment that despite some reports, Claudio Arrau had not played "the very difficult" work.

I don't believe a single person commented to me on the contretemps, not even the *Times Herald* regular music critic, who despised but feared Rosenfield. I guess if you were not in the audience for the concert and merely read about it in the morning paper you never knew the difference in what was played. Besides, Rosenfield had such a following after twenty years as *The Dallas Morning News* music critic that if any of his readers caught his error they probably blamed Claudio Arrau.

Like Mother Like Son

The courthouse square in Weatherford, Texas—before it fell victim to an unnecessarily large parking lot—had a giant model watermelon gracing the wide lawn at the east end of the tall and lovely Parker County limestone courthouse. Parker County was famous across Texas for its big, its *huge*, red-meated watermelons. Every year prizes were given to the farmer who brought the biggest melon into town. Come summer, the Farmers Market at Weatherford and the Bankhead Highway entering and leaving the city were lined with wa-

Larry Hagman.
He had his own Texas money.

termelon stands, and you could buy a forty- or fifty-pounder for one cent a pound hot, or two cents a pound cold—from galvanized tin water troughs full of ice.

But sometime in the 1950s the gods of agribusiness decreed that watermelons should be no bigger than a soccer ball, that beefsteak tomatoes, with their delicious acidy taste and enormous size, should be outlawed, and that cantaloupes must not be sold without at least one-half inch of green rind. So, the market for big watermelons disappeared, along with Weatherford's big model watermelon on the courthouse square. However, by this time Weatherford had gained a new source of pride—Mary Martin.

Judge Preston Martin's vivacious daughter, Mary, married young lawyer Ben Hagman and the Depression hit just as they had their first child, a boy, Larry. Mary, full of energy, opened a circuit of dance studios around West Texas. But despite a reasonable amount of success, she was unhappy. She wanted to *do*, not teach. One summer she left husband and son, went to Dallas, and gained a place with the outdoor Starlight Operetta, quickly made it to Broadway where, in 1938, she appeared in *Leave It to Me*, and stopped the show singing Cole Porter's "My Heart Belongs to Daddy." Shortly after she divorced Ben Hagman. She became an international star and in 1953 when she appeared in *Peter Pan*, the role became hers, and vice versa. Weatherford regained its local pride. Several years ago a statue of Mary Martin as Peter Pan was substituted for the late lamented big watermelon on the courthouse square.

Her son Larry gained his own kind of theatrical fame, working in movies and starring in television. When the TV series *Dallas* made Larry Hagman and his villainous character, J. R. Ewing, major citizens of the City of Dallas, the whole world watched. His wife, Maj, said one year she and Larry Hagman walked into a Columbia Broadcasting System board meeting, and the entire room rose and applauded. The chairman, reading the successful annual report, said, "We owe it all to Dallas . . . J. R. Ewing's *Dallas* that Larry gives us (laughter) . . . for a small sum (more laughter) . . . and to Tom Landry's Dallas Cowboy football team."

When *Dallas* was in town filming, Larry Hagman was feted and feasted every night. (He didn't drink liquor and one day a week was "silence day"—he refused to speak.) I had a chance encounter with Larry Hagman at the wedding of Fred and Jerrie Smith's daughter, Jennie, where Hagman caught the bride's blue garter with the walking stick he was carrying at the time. When I was introduced to him I remarked that we were the only two West Texans at the reception, and we chatted about Weatherford, his mother's dance studios, and his birth. I said I knew he was born in Weatherford, but he corrected me. "I was born in Fort Worth." I was bemused; every reference I had seen listed Weatherford as his birthplace.

"Why were you born in Fort Worth?" I inquired. "Because my mother was there," he said, in his best J. R. Ewing voice. Then he explained that in 1931 his mother, Mary Martin, was pregnant but didn't want to have the baby in Weatherford for hospital reasons, you might say. So the eighteen-year-old girl deliberately accepted party invitations to Fort Worth—about twenty miles east of Weatherford—and sure enough, one night she had to be rushed from a party straight to a Fort Worth hospital, and Larry was there born.

Even in some 1990s editons of *Who's Who in America*, and theater and film reference volumes, Larry Hagman is listed as "b. Weatherford, TX."

Selling the Deed to Dallas

*O*ne Dallas morning at about 8:30, I answered the telephone and a nasal voice addressed me. "A. C.—Ross Perot." I answered, "Good morning, Mr. Perot." I concealed my wonderment at what he could possibly want me for at 8:30 A.M. I had met Ross Perot only once at a neighborhood Christmas party.

"I have a telegram here that says I can contact you about buying the deed to the City of Dallas," Perot said.

Ross Perot

In light of his later political forays, this statement might mislead some people into thinking Ross Perot had gained secret information and was trying to use his billions to obtain the municipality where he lived. It took me a couple of seconds to realize what he was talking about—the deed in question was dated 1854. I told him I thought I could turn up the deed and we made a date for later that day. I would bring it to his home for him to look at it. (Don't get the wrong socio-economic implication from the fact, but we lived only a short distance apart.)

My friend, the late Barrot Sanders, a Dallas historian and collector, had a few weeks before told me of acquiring the Texas land grant which gave to John Neely Bryan, the founder of Dallas, 640 acres "including the town of Dallas." (Actually the grant turned out to be for only 580 acres.) Barrot was an astonishing collector and individual. He seemed to have some ancient, secret source. My son Eliot, a friend of his, was convinced Barrot was 200 years old. Barrot, who seemed to have learned a lot of shrewd trading ideas in his 200 years, brought the framed document over for my inspection. I felt that it was genuine and quite valuable.

After Ross Perot's telephone call, I contacted Barrot and he admitted he had sent telegrams to the three richest men in Dallas (his numerals) and used my name as the contact "because I knew they wouldn't pay any attention if I signed it." He brought the precious document to me and I met with Ross Perot late that afternoon, his guarded gate opening to me without my having to show an ID. He looked over the deed, asking me several questions as to why I thought it was authentic. I gave him some intricate historical proofs, and he accepted them, but wanted to know if he sent it to the history department of the University of Texas at Austin and it was found to be a fake would his money be refunded? I said, certainly. I knew that no one in the history department of the University of Texas at Austin knew the details of Dallas history (too regional) and if puzzled would probably asked me about it anyway. With that Ross Perot took out a little checkbook like women carry in their purses, and wrote a personal check for the healthy purchase price. Just like a woman paying for her weekly visit to the beauty shop. To me it was a wonderful gesture.

Next day both Dallas newspapers carried tongue-in-cheek stories on page 1, implying "Does Ross Perot now own Dallas?" I told reporters that so far as I knew, Dallas was the only major American city that had ever had one deed that covered the whole place. Perot was pleased with the reception the deed to Dallas got. He told me he got more attention from this deed than he'd gotten (a year before) when he bought an original copy of the British *Magna Charta*.

Ross Perot was, and is, very interested in history. A few years after the Dallas deed purchase, he called me again, explaining that he was to be seated next to Her Britannic Majesty, Queen Elizabeth II, at a Texas banquet in her honor and he wondered if I could tell him any historical fact that might tie Texas with England? I suggested he ask her about the Republic of Texas having an embassy in London during the 1840s after Great Britain had recognized Texas as an independent nation. He called back in a few days telling me that Queen Elizabeth hadn't known about the Texas embassy and was delighted with the information.

W. H. Auden

A Poet's Poetry

*S*ome years after I had retired as Book Editor of the *Dallas Times Herald*, I received a Saturday morning call from a poetic airline employee at Dallas Love Field who thought I was still at it. "If you want to see the world famous W. H. Auden," he told me, "better get out here. Auden's going to arrive in just a few minutes."

Of course I wanted to see Auden, the celebrated English-American poet—although I couldn't figure what he was coming to Dallas for. I knew of no poetry conference or other literary meeting scheduled in Dallas or at any of the universities in the immediate area. So, I called the late Larry Perrine, of the Southern Methodist English faculty, and author and editor of *Sound and Sense*, that handbook that has introduced two, maybe three, generations of college students to modern poetry. Larry seemed to me an appropriate colleague with whom to meet (uninvited) Wystan Hugh Auden, and he was eager to go. On the way to the airport I told Larry I had read some practitioner of the art who wrote that a poet, like a mathematician, had to do his best work before age thirty. Larry scoffed; he still wrote poetry, he said, pretty good poetry, and he was well past age thirty—and look at Auden!

Auden had arrived when we got to Love Field and we found him seated alone in a waiting room. We introduced ourselves, begged his pardon for simply walking in like this, and I asked what he was doing in Dallas. It turned out he was on his way to Shreveport, Louisiana, to address the students of a boys' school which was run by a friend of his. A private plane was suppose to pick him up in about an hour. We asked if he minded if we talked a while and he said of course not, it would keep him company. (Auden's face, as interesting as a Rembrandt etching, was the most paper-wrinkled piece of skin I have ever seen.)

Larry Perrine asked about some of the newer poets, and Auden very politely answered, but avoided making any direct comments. Larry and I both brought up our favorites of his masterworks. I had done a lengthy graduate school paper on his poetry along with that of Louis MacNeice and Stephen Spender as "poetry of the machine." But as I had made a B grade, I thought it best not to bring it up.

Auden told us of a visit to his birthplace, England, where, as an American citizen, he had to answer some personal questions. When Auden was asked, "What do you do?" he said he was a writer. The officer wrote down: "No occupation."

I mentioned that Larry was author and editor of *Sound and Sense* and Larry mentioned the Auden pieces he had included. Both of us could tell he was too polite to suggest he was unfamiliar with the book. Then I asked what he was going to speak to the boys school about and suggested he might spice up his talk with some limericks. Auden brightened and said, "What a wonderful idea." Larry said, "I compose a limerick now and then," and Auden replied, "How splendid! I do too."

At that point the art of the limerick became the topic of our conversation. Auden told us of some famous English poets, going back several years, who had written the witty little pieces, and we all agreed that only a so-called dirty limerick really qualified for the acclaim we felt for the form. Larry recited a couple of his own composition, and I contributed a couple of my favorites. Although I had left the profession at the time, when it came to limericks, I was still known in Dallas journalistic circles as "the source."

Auden's plane didn't arrive in Dallas for more than an hour. By that time Larry Perrine and I had learned a good bit of Auden lore, and Auden had learned some new limericks, tho' hardly the kind to use in a public lecture at a boys' school.

A Song and Destiny

Sometimes chance, operating in its casual way, has something bigger in store than we might have predicted in a thousand years. In my case, the moving finger began writing its delayed message one spring many, many seasons ago when I was in high school.

Although far from being of their number, I had been assigned to Study Hall D, which, almost by tradition, included a goodly tribe of sports heroes and members of the silver-spoon set—that handful of students who lived in the choicer sections of town. Study Hall D was on the third floor of the old Abilene High School building and was situated in such a way that the windows on two sides could remain open most of the spring and fall seasons, a cross breeze keeping the long room comfortable while the rest of the building sweltered in the Texas heat.

Another delight about Study Hall D was the way sound drifted up and through those open windows. People on the campus below often could be heard making amusing and interesting remarks they had no idea were being overheard. Once the entire study hall burst out in applause when a male teacher, far down at our feet, was heard informing an adult colleague that a certain lad, who was in Study Hall D at that moment, "was a little turd." The study hall teacher hastily lowered the windows through which the talk was entering, but too late. (The "little turd" later became a mathematician and contributed to the development of the computer.)

At approximately 2 P.M., several times a month, another, more dulcet, sound floated up to us as Bryce Jordan, the first chair flutist of the AHS orchestra, left orchestra practice and strolled across our corner of the campus sweetly blowing passages from whatever music the orchestra was undertaking. Jimmy Atkinson, a notable vocalist, my closest friend and Study Hall D'er, dubbed Bryce "the wandering flautist." (How can you chart destiny? Bryce, after years as a widely heralded musicologist, turned to academics and became president of the University of Texas at Dallas, then was president of Penn State from 1983 until retiring in 1990. Jimmy also left music to teach, and retired as Dean of Foreign Students at Pepperdine University.)

Located just across the street from the high school, was another institution that serenaded us even more frequently than the wandering flautist. This was the juke box at the student hangout named "The Pollyana Shop." The Pollyana was very upscale and very upperclassman. I didn't dare enter the front door until I was a junior. To show you how upscale it was, hamburgers at the Pollyana were a dime, not the customary nickel. I never smoked, but cigarettes could be bought for five cents a piece, which drew a lot of the "don't you ever let me catch you with a cigarette in your mouth, young man (or young lady)!" trade.

The Pollyana juke box, as you might expect, carried the best and the latest big band records. It played continuously during the noon hour, the silver-spoon set supplying the nickels. I played the Pollyana juke box only twice—both times with slugs. These had their centers punched out but if you carefully wrapped a paper soda straw so as to cover the hole the slug would buy you music.

That juke box entertained Study Hall D every day. The Pollyana's owner had a handful of nickels with identifying red paint on them that he used to "prime" the juke box if too much silence occurred. The music came our way so clearly that occasionally the teacher would have to warn the students to quit humming.

One afternoon, as I was lazily deciding whether to be a lawyer or a poet when I grew up, suddenly I heard the Pollyana juke box pouring out a stunning stream of music. It was Artie Shaw's recording of "Begin the Beguine" and I was hearing it for the first time. By virtue of my parents' half-inch thick Edison platters and their 1920s and 1930s shellacs, I had gained an appreciation for the old jazz. But this song was different. It spoke to me personally, Shaw's clarinet discovering something powerful for me—my own sixteen-year-old soul music. The years may have made this too romantic a memory, but when "Begin the Beguine" stopped, I wasn't the same boy as the one who had been sitting there four minutes before.

It turned Artie Shaw's life around, too. The first day his recording of "Begin the Beguine" was released it lifted him into the kind of continuing fame no public relations department or promotion scheme can accomplish. Although the late Cole Porter composed "Begin the Beguine," Artie Shaw's arrangement is so well known that even Porter laughingly admitted most people thought Artie Shaw had written it. Not to imply that "Begin the Beguine" was the only classic Shaw made. I won't list the two dozen or more of his recordings that are heard every day on some radio station. Few of his recordings have aged.

After that afternoon in Study Hall D, I was an Artie Shaw fan, spending my newspaper route nickels and dimes for his recordings, sometimes able to get them for only a dime after they came off a juke box (the A side scratchy the B side usually unplayed!) But I was willing, when able, to pay thirty-five cents for a new Victor recording. By the time Shaw introduced strings to his band I had subscribed to *Down Beat*, a monthly swing trade magazine. I listened as well to Benny Goodman, Glenn Miller, Tommy Dorsey and a number of other bands—crouched until midnight by my cathedral-top Crossley radio, as two or three of the better known bands played from glamorous places like Frank Daly's Meadowbrook, New York's Pennsylvania Hotel, or Chicago's Edgewater Beach Hotel. But it was Shaw I followed most faithfully on and off the bandstand. For instance, he rescued a woman from drowning at Acapulco, and I shrugged off his marital adventures—so many marriages to so many famous beauties. It was his music I coveted, not his wives.

Going into the Navy, I told my family I wanted Artie Shaw to play at my funeral, and if he couldn't make it, play his recording of "Chantez le bas."

Then, an adult at last, married, in the retail book business, I read his first book, *The Trouble with Cinderella*, and found a more profound man than I had expected, and I also began to understand the connection between the musician as an artist and the musician as a harried human. I pushed his book to music lover and psychiatry and psychology followers alike. And I never had a complaint from any of them.

Then early in 1965 came the possibility mentioned earlier—that sometimes chance has something in store for us which we couldn't predict in a thousand years. I was wearing my book editor's hat at the *Dallas Times Herald* when I answered the phone. A crisp secretarial voice asked if I was the Book Editor of the *Dallas Times Herald*, and I agreed I was. "Will you hold, please, for Mr. Artie Shaw," the crisp voice asked. I knew at once this was the sort of joke staff friends like Dick Hitt or Gary Cartwright, knowing of my devotion to Shaw, were not only capable of pulling but likely to, especially if they had located another person named Artie Shaw or had been able to line up an impersonator.

I agreed to speak with "Mr. Artie Shaw," looking around to see if anyone in the news room was snickering or casting too many amused glances in my direction. But it was Artie Shaw calling from New York. He asked if my wife and I could have dinner with him one night next week. I couldn't say "Of course" quickly enough. I asked why he called me—I wasn't in the entertainment or music department. He called me because I was book editor and he had a new book coming out. "I've made my clarinet into a lamp stand," he said, a reply he often used to explain that he had retired from playing. I told him I had been a Shaw fan for years, but he brushed it aside. He wasn't in the "Artie Shaw business," as he later insisted.

Our meeting was a great success. Artie Shaw was a film distributor at the time and he set up a viewing for Betty and me of a picture he was handling, *Seance on a Wet Afternoon*, a British film with Richard Attenborough that has become a cult film, and next week he sent me advance proofs of his fiction collection: *I Love You, I Hate You, Drop Dead*. At another time Artie and I talked of doing a screenplay about the Kennedy assassination, using New Orleans as a major setting—predating Oliver Stone's *JFK* by twenty years.

Contrary to most of my chance encounters, this one did not end with one or two meetings. Artie Shaw has remained a close and valued friend. He is an innovative writer, a gifted musician, a philosopher, and probably the smartest man I've met, certainly the best read—but that is the public side of him. I know a much warmer, more inspiring person, a thoughtful man with an informed opinion on virtually everything from modern music, classical and popular, to the hereafter—opinions readily expressed. Once, as a panel member, he says he was rather outspoken and afterward a man from the audience said to him, "Mr. Shaw, you sure missed a lot of opportunities to be quiet." I am pleased to say that in thirty-six years, Artie Shaw and I have never had a serious disagreement, although we certainly have differing opinions on many matters.

George T. Simon, a music historian, wrote of him, "He was a much deeper thinker than most band leaders; a man concerned with and constantly analyzing his place and the place of his music in [our] society." Gary Theroux, a *Reader's Digest* music critic, commented, "Artie was never an easy man to get along with. Touchy, outspoken and opinionated, he had little time for autograph hounds . . . the musically ignorant, folks who requested the same hits over and over, and the music business itself." In 2000, his ninetieth year, a thirteen-part radio series covering his life was titled "The Mystery of Artie Shaw." Although the series was a tribute to the man, the "mystery" was how to interpret the many changes in direction of his life. To me the so-called mystery is very simple: Artie Shaw is always trying to expand his knowledge and his intellectual boundaries. For instance, as he passed his ninety-first birthday he was busy working with a New York editor on a huge (1200 manuscript pages) semi-autobiographical novel about a musician growing up in the jazz and swing era.

You never fail to learn something from Artie Shaw if a name, an idea or a news event is brought up. The last of the *big* big band leaders, he met everybody, it seems, in music and Hollywood, but also people like Ernest Hemingway, a Shaw fan, who took Artie pub-crawling in New York after Hemingway discovered Artie had read all his books. I mentioned Bix Biederbecke, the legendary trumpet player, and Artie said he had roomed with him. He also has a private sort of courtliness which has charmed both my wives, as well as a few hundred others. How could I have guessed, that afternoon in Study Hall D when I first heard those familiar opening notes of "Begin the Beguine," that I was taking first steps toward one of my closest friendships, one that would endure for decades?

Chance Encounters
During the Turbulent Dallas Days

Lee Harvey Oswald holds a
Mannlicher Carcano rifle and
newspaper in a backyard in
Dallas, Texas.

Ann Richards

"Get Us Out!" Gets Me a Political Friend

Early in 1963 I was made Editor of the Editorial Page at the *Dallas Times Herald*, taking over the page from a man who had been a charter member of the local John Birch Society. In case the John Birch Society is unfamiliar, it was a fervid national anti-communist movement which spotted Reds wholesale and had it in for the United Nations. The much advertised slogan, "Get U.S. Out of U.N.," was of John Birch origin.

At the time I was appointed Editor I had little inclination toward political argle-bargle, but at that period you couldn't be neutral in Dallas. The city was kept upset by various right-wing groups who avowed they were fighting communism by putting "Impeach Earl Warren" stickers on empty store fronts. I think the very fact that my political persuasions were unknown helped get me the job. But as noted, neutrality wouldn't work: he who is not dedicated 100% for us, is 100% against us! Within days of my taking over the editorial page there were howls a-plenty, but there were letters welcoming the change: "Like a fresh breeze . . ." and "Thank God, a sane voice." Overnight the *Dallas Times Herald* became one of the few major newspaper in Texas not leaning toward, or falling into, the conservative rut.

Our pages began to gain humane characteristics that had been missing before, although the Warren "impeachers" and the anti-UN'ers missed those old thrilling warnings, "They're only 90 miles away!" Of course, the wild predictions kept on coming. One of my favorites arrived by way of a woman who wrote to chastise me that while I was "fooling around with the liberals" the communists had invaded our shores. She wrote, "Did you know there are 30,000 uniformed Red Chinese troops in Baja, California!"

Very early as editor I had an interesting encounter which led to a continuing friendship. One morning when I answered my telephone a sort of husky female voice asked me, without preliminaries, "Who th' hell are you?" I tried to explain that I was just a reporter who had been made Editorial Page Editor.

"I don't mean that," she said, "I mean, where are you from? How did you ever get the job of being Editorial Page Editor in Dallas?" I told her I was from Abilene and she laughed, "My god, Abilene's holier than Waco, where I'm from." We chatted on amiably for a while, with me rather prissily informing her that I was riding neither Donkey nor Elephant when I was writing editorials. Even from a brief telephone conversation I could tell she was a sharp-witted, sagacious political observer—fervently Democratic. I invited her down to meet my little staff in person, and she accepted.

When the female voice came in my office two days later I saw a beautiful blonde woman, her good looks set off dramatically by a bright red suit, who introduced herself as Ann Richards. We conferred over Cokes in the coffee shop for an hour—not without good humored friction—and I knew that ultimately this powerful personality would be rewarded, as indeed it was several years later when Ann Richards capped a political career by becoming Governor of the State of Texas.

Hunting For H. L. Hunt

One of the first things my friends outside Dallas wanted to know when I took over the *Times Herald* editorial page was: "What are you going to do about H. L. Hunt?" It was more a challenge than a question.

Of course, I understood in a general way what my friends meant:

H. L. Hunt

they, like millions of others, thought that H. L. Hunt was surely the most powerful man in Dallas, his unseen hand stirring every political pot or plot, ready to jerk you off your job or run you out of your political office if you went *mano a mano* with him. How else could it be, living in the town with someone who supported an entire industry of right-wing thinking.

But, I asked, what was a $175 a week newspaper editor supposed to do about the person *Life* magazine had implied was "The Richest Man in the U. S."?

Well, by the time I was appointed editor I had already discovered that H. L. Hunt had none of the local clout outsiders credited him with having. Quaint? To be sure. I once told Robert Sherrill, who was writing for *The Nation*, that H. L. Hunt would be the most dangerous man in America "if he weren't such a damn hick." It was a kind of smart-alecky statement, but it was true. Hunt had millions with which he could have bought mass circulation newspapers, radio and television stations—maybe even a network—but what did he do? He paid for production of an amateurish radio program called "Life Line" and a couple of klunky television shows named "Answers for Americans" and "State of the Nation." He published a "Facts Forum" anti-communist newsletter that surely made the Kremlin insiders laugh, if they ever saw it.

Hunt might have been a shrewd (or lucky) gambler, but he never understood politics. In the 1960 presidential race he went to the Democratic convention in Los Angeles and tried to buy in with a laughable $20,000 contribution. Neither Johnson nor Kennedy, vying for the nomination, would accept his money.

New York intellectuals seemed to have been the most convinced that H. L. Hunt was an awesome power, protected by bunches of secretaries, body guards and lawyers. Once a frantic Manhattan publishing company's publicity director called me (because I was also book editor) and told me, excitedly, that H. L. Hunt had bought *The Saturday Review of Literature*. Would I call him and dare to ask? I told her that H. L. Hunt was easy to contact, that he often answered his own phone, but that I doubted he had bought *The Saturday Review* unless he had taken it in along with some bigger corporate deal, the way another Texas millionaire had obtained *Sports Afield* magazine. But my New York friend was afraid to call Hunt. She was afraid he might try to get her job, she said. I finally said I would ask Mr. Hunt if he had bought *The Saturday Review*.

I called his office and got him quickly. I told him that New York was wanting me to ask him if he had bought *The Saturday Review of Literature*. He paused, and I could immediately tell the name of the magazine had fallen on uncomprehending ears.

"Maybe I have and maybe I haven't," he said.

"Have you made a recent trade that might have included this magazine without your knowing it?" I asked.

His reply, "Maybe I have and maybe I haven't."

I finally told him, "Mr. Hunt, I don't think you have bought *The Saturday Review* and I'm going to tell New York you haven't. Is that all right?"

He said, philosophically, "Maybe it is and maybe it isn't."

I called back to New York and told my friend that I was certain H. L. Hunt had not bought *The Saturday Review*. She offered her best piece of evidence: "Well, Hunt Foods is now the owner, and that's H. L. Hunt, isn't it?"

I was relieved. "You're safe. Hunt Foods is owned by Norton Simon, the California art collector and oilman. H. L. Hunt's food company is HLH Products and isn't a drop in the bucket compared to Hunt Foods." She, and (I suppose) the New York publishing world, were greatly relieved.

As editorial page editor, I regularly received mail from Hunt discussing various national problems, or solutions to problems as he saw them. They were not full of political paranoia, but were similar to the lines of his paperback novel, *Alpaca*, a republic where university graduates were given as many as seven votes. *Alpaca* had aroused much tea-cup furor among those who had not read it. His letters also came too frequently for us to use each one. We had a list of "constant readers" whose letters we had to ration to three or four-week appearances. H. L. Hunt was one of those. As his missives were much too long for newspaper use, I had to chop it down when one was used, ripping through paragraphs in an attempt to let him say what I thought he was wanting to say.

One morning I got a phone call and a quiet voice said, "Mr. Greene, this is H. L. Hunt." You never knew what H. L. Hunt might want to discuss, but I said, "How can I help you?"

"Mr. Greene," he said, "what is your salary for a year?"

I laughed, "Mr. Hunt, are you trying to get me fired? You can't ask a newspaperman how much he makes. All I can tell you is, I don't think I make as much as you."

He very earnestly continued, "Well, Mr. Greene, I spend quite a bit of time composing letters to you, then I have one of my lawyers look them over, and then my secretary types them out—and she's a good 'un. Makes five dollars an hour." I said that, yes, I had noticed the quality of the typing.

He continued, "Then I mail the letters to you, and much of the time you don't run them, and when you do you rewrite them."

I tried to explain that we didn't rewrite anyone's letters, but as our Editor's Notice pointed out, all letters were subject to editing for size.

"But Mr. Greene," he said, "By the time I pay my secretary to type the letter, and my lawyer, who makes a great deal more than my secretary, to read it—and my own time's worth a little something—and you cut them up or don't run them, I figure you are costing me $50,000 a year, and I just wondered if you made that much?"

I assured H. L. Hunt that I didn't make $50,000 a year and added I was sorry he wrote so many letters if the cost was so high. I didn't think it was worth it. He made some kind of polite statement and I thanked him and said goodbye.

Shortly after President Kennedy's assassination (which hundreds of journalists *just knew* H. L. Hunt had a hand in) a magazine writer called me and asked, very seriously, "Have you been told that after the assassination, H. L. Hunt spent all night riding around crouched down in the back seat of his chauffeur-driven Cadillac, scared to go home?" I asked why he was scared. "His co-conspirators threatened to kill him because Lee Harvey Oswald had been taken alive. Hunt finally got Jack Ruby to do the job."

I told the magazine writer that I knew one thing wrong in that scenario: H. L. Hunt didn't drive a Cadillac. "He nearly hit me coming out of an underground parking garage the other day driving his Oldsmobile."

Nevertheless, I called Mr. Hunt at his office and while I didn't go into details, asked if he'd spent that night riding crouched in the back seat of his chauffeur-driven Cadillac. H. L. Hunt gave an uncharacteristicly short answer: "I don't have a chauffeur.

With Adlai, Gladly

*E*arly in October, 1963, I received a letter with no name on the outside of the envelope—merely a return address. I recognized it as the Dallas United Nations organization headquarters. The reason it was so recognizable was the notoriety connected with the address; not because of anything the Dallas United Nations organization had done but what had been done to the Dallas United Nations organiza-

Adlai Stevenson,
U. S. Ambassador to the United Nations.

tion—broken windows, graffiti, hundreds of anti-United Nations signs. The fact that most of the turmoil involved only a few hundred Dallasites seems beside the point. It was dangerous to flaunt your sympathy for, much less your association with the United Nations Organization, Dallas branch.

The letter contained an invitation from Mr. Stanley Marcus and Mr. Robert Storey, Sr., which requested "the pleasure of your company at a luncheon in honor of His Excellency, Mr. Adlai E. Stevenson, Ambassador Extraordinary and Plenipotentiary of the United States to the United Nations on United Nations Day, Thursday, the twenty-fourth of October at twelve o'clock . . . Sheraton-Dallas Hotel."

Today it is difficult to credit the furor that the slightest favorable mention of the United Nations raised at that time. Recognizing this, I was surprised when the vice president of the *Dallas Times Herald*, Jim Chambers, called me to ask if I had received an invitation to the luncheon to meet Adlai Stevenson and was I planning on going? I said I had certainly planned on it, since I believed it was something of a historical necessity to meet Ambassador Stevenson. Chambers then surprised me by not only saying he was going, but asking if I wanted to accompany him. "I can't get any of the old heads to go with me. I think they're afraid to be seen with Stevenson," he said. My surprise was not at Chambers's political view being counter to what I expected, it was that Chambers was offering to take me with him. He seldom fraternized with the hired help—other than to play golf from time to time with sports writer Dan Jenkins, who had been Southwest Conference champion at Texas Christian University a few years before.

But I must give Jim Chambers credit for foreseeing that the political course Dallas seemed to be taking was dangerous. Earlier that year he had been in a White House press conference between a group of national newspaper publishers and President John F. Kennedy where the rival Dallas publisher, the late E. M. (Ted) Dealey of *The Dallas Morning News*, had blasted JFK telling him to "get off Caroline's tricycle," what the people wanted was "a man on horseback."

President Kennedy was furious, and Chambers, after the meeting, apologized to him and assured him that Dealey—who was famous for his outspokenness—did not speak for Dallas. The President turned to an aide and said, "Let's drop the other paper and take this man's." Chambers returned to Dallas and wrote a blistering account of the White House meeting, naming the rival publisher and the paper by name—something unheard of in Dallas.

After the Kennedy assassination nearly every journalist who came to Dallas—and they came by the hundreds—either quoted *The Morning News* first or batched the two papers together in gauging Dallas's "atmosphere." The truth is, *The Morning News* had at that time a wonderfully convenient library—the *Times Herald* had none, so the press corp spent more time across town from us at *The Morning News*.

Jim Chambers had a new Lincoln automobile, so he, Stevenson and a local UN supporter and I rode around Dallas visiting important individuals who were at least amenable to the United Nations idea. As we rode I didn't do much of the talking, although Chambers once pointed out, "A. C.'s got the Right-Wingers all over him."

As we were going into the hotel where the Ambassador was to speak, Chambers surprised me further when he told me he believed the United Nations was "our best hope for peace." It was not the kind of thing most of the *Times Herald* higher-ups would announce.

During the Stevenson speech I was flattered when I heard the Ambassador quote me at one point. It had been an interesting morning and Adlai Stevenson was not only capable of great humor but had a political vision that didn't always get out—or was not allowed to get out—during his failed presidential campaigns.

The Ambassador returned to his hotel room after a prolonged lunch and I went back to my office to mull over a column I had in mind about Stevenson. That night as he began his United Nations Day speech at the Memorial Auditorium, all hell broke loose. A group of about seventy-five hecklers tried, with a good bit of success, to break it up. Adlai Stevenson stood there for nearly twenty minutes, unbelieving, unable even with the mechanical aid of the microphone, to complete a sentence, while the weird fury roared before him. He tried humor—"I believe in the forgiveness of sin and the redemption of ignorance," he told the audience—then common decency; finally he was eloquently pleading in a mute stance for just the chance to finish a thought. Although the capacity audience was overwhelmingly for the Ambassador, nothing availed until the police moved in and bodily removed the invaders.

Eventually order was restored and Adlai Stevenson began to speak unimpeded, but about that time a huge sign, stage right of the Memorial Auditorium theater, originally reading "Welcome Adlai," suddenly flipped down, with a roar, to read: "UN Red Front." General Edwin Walker had made an anti-UN speech in the same hall the night before at a "U. S. Day" rally—Oswald claimed to have been there—but the general denied he or his organization had anything to do with the disruptive sign. I think it was the work of a hastily formed Dallas group which styled itself "The National Indignation Convention." The sign caper was just the sort of juvenile mischief these people were capable of doing. (The NIC disappeared immediately after the Kennedy assassination.)

Following the speech, Adlai Stevenson had to run a gauntlet of jeering, shoving foes as he was being escorted to a waiting limousine sent to carry him back to the hotel. One twenty-two-year-old man actually spat on him. Just as he reached the limousine, a woman, tongue extended, reached out with a cardboard placard on a stick and took an awkward lunge which reached the Ambassador. She also hit Val Imm, a *Times Herald* Woman's Page columnist who was shaking Adlai Stevenson's hand and apologizing to him for "those people's" behavior. The police immediately seized the woman, but the Ambassador quickly waved off her arrest. (While neither Adlai Stevenson nor Val was injured, the sign, if it had struck some sensitive facial area, could have been quite damaging.)

Ambassador Stevenson simply could not believe what was taking place. He said later that this had been the first time "in my experience" anything like this had happened. He sat in the back seat of the limousine while the attackers still swarmed around the car. He was wide-eyed with dismay, his attacker's saliva actually dripping down one cheek, and he choked out his thoughts:

"Animals . . . animals. They are like animals . . . they don't hear."

It was a tumultuous time, but what has not been noted very often is that the majority of the crowd was supporting the Ambassador and some of those members had to be restrained from attacking the so-called protesters.

I had left the gathering at the Memorial Auditorium before the spitting attack. Johnny Weeks had stayed to the ugly end, and he phoned me at home in outrage, almost screaming to me, "You've got to write something . . . we've got to let the world know this isn't us."

I wrote what was, and is still termed, the strongest local editorial ever to appear in a modern Dallas newspaper. I called down to the City Editor early the next morning and told him to run it "pI" (page 1). He protested I didn't have the status to order something run pI, but I said I would take the heat, if the action created any—and threatened to have heat put on him if he refused. He finally agreed. After our strongly worded editorial had appeared on the front page— indicating it spoke for the entire *Dallas Times Herald* administration, not just the editorial page—the Dallas City Council and the leaders of the community were aroused to take action against similar out-breaks. This was before such actions became common on university campuses, and even the most conservative of the *Times Herald* bosses told me they approved of my demand it be front page.

The howling attack on Stevenson represented the highest tide of right-wing fanaticism in Dallas. I am convinced if Dallas had not be-come the scene of the Kennedy assassination, within a few months it would have been able to rid itself of the outspoken far-right fanatics. They were never near a majority. And with Adlai Stevenson's dis-graceful treatment, even the most conservative of the city's leaders was determined Dallas's "ultra" reputation had to be erased. By the time of the visit of President Kennedy, this realization was at work, purging the civic body of the sickness.

The criticism of Dallas following the assassination was emotional and, as time has proved, unfounded in its accusations that Dallas was implicated in that tragic act. But the attack on Adlai Stevenson was something else, and Dallas knew it and recognized what it meant: we had looked away while the fanatics were taking us too far.

Despite having been quoted by *The New York Times* and other newspapers over the nation after it appeared on October 25, 1963, in the frenzy of accusation that Dallas was "a city of hate," this editorial was overlooked by those who insisted both Dallas newspapers had been blindly "Far-Right."

Dallas Disgrace

Dallas has been disgraced. There is no other way to view the stormtrooper actions of last night's frightening attack on Adlai Stevenson.

Must our city gain the reputation around the world of being a place where a guest is physically endangered if he expresses any idea of which a belligerent, minority mob disapproves?

The senseless inability of some of the residents of Dallas to tolerate those with whom they disagree is the very opposite of democracy. And this misconstrued, misguided brand of "patriotism" is dragging the name of Dallas through the slime of national dishonor.

This is not political, it is psychotic. It is the sick mania of intolerance, the frenzied fear of self-delusion. Thursday night's jeering, bullying mob was not attacking the United Nations; it was battling the right of you and me to hold our separate beliefs and the right of any man to express any belief. What we as individuals think about the United Nations matters not one whit. What we think about freedom is endangered terribly.

The decent, sincere political organizations of Dallas, the leadership of our city, must speak out and repudiate these fringe elements before greater disaster is wrought on the face of the place we love and live in. It is irresponsible to the point of criminality on the part of any organ or organization which, by failing to denounce such brown-shirt action, condones it. It is time for the voice of the responsible, intelligent, level-headed and proud citizens of Dallas to cry out loud and clear, telling the world and this unruly handful of citizens that things have gone too far.

It is time for a sensible, modern, tolerant city to come to its senses and protect itself.

"Call After Five"

$\mathcal{O}$ur policy on the *Dallas Times Herald* editorial page was to carry as many letters to the editor as possible—even crank letters—and we didn't pick and choose among crank topics. We did try to screen out the nut letters—almost a full time job because they came streaming in from all over the U. S. The *Times Herald* was on every right-wing (or left-wing) organization's mailing list. We were careful to keep some kind of philosophical balance between "pros" and "anti's" on any question—if there was a pro- and or anti-side—occasionally offering our own italic footnote if a letter writer went too far off the rails.

And we had to be careful. Political nuts weren't the only kind of nuts who wrote to the editor. Some were more vicious. One day a Postal Inspector appeared in our office and announced he had received information we were running a pornography ring. A Dallas woman contacted him that she had sent a letter to the editor and although we hadn't run it, she immediately started receiving nasty, suggestive sex letters. She (and apparently the Postal Inspector) thought we were selling female-written letters to sex-starved males, else how had they gotten her address? We almost hated to disappoint the smug Postal Inspector by showing him that we *had* printed the woman's letter—which had nothing to do with sex—and when printed carried no address except "Dallas." We suggested, to the Postal Inspector, that there were such things as telephone directories with street addresses, and had he seen any of the "nasty, suggestive sex letters" she said she had received? Yes, he had. One of them said, "You're screwy." He and the woman both caught the sexual hint. He left our office, without apologizing, seemingly convinced he'd just smashed a porn ring. Johnny Weeks, an associate editor, wanted to call the Post Office and lodge a complaint but I said no, it might get him a promotion.

Some things received were physically impossible to accommodate: I was sent—to me personally, not as editor—a roll of toilet paper from Fort Campbell, Kentucky, with a short note, "You stink," signed "Co. B 143 Inf. Bn." [pseudonumerical]. The roll had been used, apparently by the entire company. I read over some of my columns but could find nothing worth so much effort.

Sometime in October of 1963, we received a handwritten letter that demanded "Fair Play for Cuba." It was a rambly sort of letter, not making much point other than to demand we Americans quit picking on Cuba. The letter was signed "O. H. Lee" and an Oak Cliff (Dallas) address and a telephone number were given, as required, with a note: "Call after 5." (We checked out all Letters to the Editor we thought we might use, making sure of the writer's identity and that he or she had actually written the letter.)

Ordinarily we wouldn't check on a run-of-the-page letter with a "call after 5" note, since the staff had generally proofread the next day's page and gone home by 4 or 4:30 P.M. But I decided we should follow up on this. We didn't get many messages openly favorable to Cuba. Johnny Weeks volunteered to stay with me until after five so we could call on the letter writer. We always had two persons on the telephone when we were verifying letters. At about 5:10 (with Johnny at another phone) I dialed the number and when a man answered I told him my name and said I was editorial page editor of the *Dallas Times Herald*. I asked if he were O. H. Lee and he said he was.

"Did you write us a letter recently?" I asked.

He said, "You're not going to run it, are you?"

"What was it about?" I asked, needing to make certain it was the Fair Play for Cuba letter.

"You're not going to run it," the man again replied.

I tried to explain that I was merely checking that he had written us a letter, and it hadn't come from someone with a similar name.

"It was about Fair Play for Cuba," he said, grudgingly, and added, "you're not going to run it, are you?"

I said that I couldn't guarantee that any letter would be run, we received too many. But the contents of the letter didn't bother us—in fact, we liked to receive letters on "the other side" of controversial matters. With that the whine in his voice turned obliging. He told me the *Times Herald* editorial page was his favorite: "It is fairer to the public than the other paper."

He tried to get me to promise his letter would run by a certain date, but I told him I simply couldn't promise. He seemed disappointed. He didn't subscribe to the *Times Herald*, he said, but bought it from a coin box, and it was pretty costly to have to buy a paper every afternoon not knowing when or if your letter was going to run. But he seemed happy by the time Johnny and I hung up.

It was shortly after noon on the day of the Kennedy assassination that Robert Ford, of the Associated Press office (in the *Times Herald* building) discovered O. H. Lee was one of Lee Harvey Oswald's many pseudonyms. Thus, it was Lee Harvey Oswald that Johnny and I had talked with.

I remain convinced that when Lee Harvey Oswald shot President Kennedy he was seeking attention. He kept trying to find it, and kept failing to get it. Would it have helped if I had made more over his controversial letter, maybe put a box around it to draw attention to it, or run it with a title like "Letter of the Week"? I doubt it. It hadn't helped when he was interviewed in New Orleans after his "Fair Play for Cuba" brawl. No, none of this "Man on the Street" radio stuff or mere "Letters to the Editor" was enough for Lee Harvey Oswald. It had to be *bigger*. It had to make him the Most Important Person in the World. Even if he had to die from it.

In the years since the Kennedy assassination I have told many people that anyone who has been in the daily newspaper business for five years met many "Lee Harvey Oswalds"—unknown people who were so desperate for notice they would, without hesitation, murder a famous figure even if certain death were the consequence. It is worth that moment—that supreme moment of fame—when all the world is looking at me, with hatred, maybe, but seeing *me*, by God, *me*. (Remember the triumphant look on Oswald's face when he told a television reporter, "I didn't do nothing"?)

I think Lee Harvey Oswald killed President Kennedy because he wanted to be noticed by the world and, suddenly, here was the greatest opportunity he would ever get. I also think he wanted to be caught. I think he enjoyed the power of anonymity for those first minutes, to be the invisible man, through superior cunning to play hide-and-seek in full sight—but that game was too easy. He was tired of being O. H. Lee and A. J. Hidell; he wanted to become Lee Harvey Oswald. I think he acted alone. I believe if he had been part of a conspiracy he might easily have escaped the scene—he *did* escape the assassination site—and might have fled Dallas.

What happened to the "O. H. Lee" letter? It was handwritten, and the typographers' union wouldn't set handwritten letters so when we received one we had to type a copy and send it, along with the original, to the composing room to be set—this was in the "hot metal" days of typesetting. After the letters were set in type the original and the typewritten copy were spiked on a big hook (literally) that hung in the composing room and after about three weeks the hook became full and was "cleaned." The day of the assassination, as soon as the identity of "O. H. Lee" was known, Johnny Weeks went tearing down to the composing room to go through the letters still on the copy spike, but, alas, the spike had long since been cleaned and O. H. Lee's letter demanding fair play for Cuba had been destroyed weeks before. What a loss—but then, who was to know how much history it contained?

A Free Meal at the Carousel Club

One noon I was heading for the Press Club in downtown Dallas to have lunch when I ran into Orville McDonald, whom I had known in college but hadn't seen in several years. After we had caught up somewhat on histories, he asked me if I was meeting anyone for lunch and I said I wasn't.

"Let me buy you a meal," he said. "I have a client you should meet."

Orville was one of those entrepreneurs who appear in your life every so often, then disappear for months, or years, at a time. I once asked him what he did for a living—he lived very well—and he said, "I don't really know how to describe it." I knew it wasn't illegal, so I didn't persist.

This was well before the Kennedy assassination and the meal he offered was at Jack Ruby's Carousel Club. Orville said Ruby was trying to sell the club and, as a favor, he was helping him. I was familiar with Jack Ruby's name and had heard all kinds of stories about his temper and his in-and-out reputation—nearly every Dallas newspaper reporter had. The problem was, you might say, the sleaze factor. Ruby wasn't a police or underworld character, but I wasn't too eager to enter the Carousel Club, even for a free meal. But Orville assured me that at noon it was simply a quiet place where we could also get a drink.

The Carousel Club was up some stairs in the second story over a retail establishment. It was not a glamorous site. As is nearly always the case with a night club in day time, it had a tired, tawdry look to it. As I recall, a bandstand had a set of drums showing, plus a zipped up acoustic bass, but the noontime music was canned. I don't remember if there were others there, but surely there were. Orville ordered the meal and I had a bottle of beer with mine. As we were eating the proprietor came over and Orville introduced me to him. Jack Ruby shook my hand and asked me about several reporters, mainly those assigned to the cop shop (police station). I knew most of them, and having passed the test, I suppose, Mr. Ruby took out one of his business cards and wrote, "Good for one free drink at the Carousel Club," signed his name and handed it to me. "Next time you're thirsty, come on up," he said, "and bring old George Carter with you." George Carter was the *Times Herald's* veteran police writer. George knew every character in town, including those who *were* police and underworld characters. I thanked Jack Ruby, although I was pretty sure I wouldn't be cashing in on the free drink. (Texas law then didn't allow public sale of mixed drinks so you had to be a member of a club or bring your own bottle to get hard liquor.)

That meeting took place before I became Editorial Page Editor and I had no occasion to see Jack Ruby. And the Carousel Club didn't sell. But one afternoon, when I had been the editor for six months or so, Don Safran, our night club writer, came into my office with Jack Ruby and asked if I had a few minutes; "Jack wants to ask you something." I shook hands again with Mr. Ruby and reminded him we had already met by means of Orville McDonald. He remembered Orville but may not have remembered me.

I asked him what he wanted to ask. He said, "I want you to write an editorial about my exotic."

I hesitated a moment, then asked him, "What has she done?" (I was reasonably sure his "exotic" was female.)

"She has a college education," Ruby said, "and that's damn rare in an exotic. I've handled hundreds of 'em and this is the first one with a college education."

Jack Ruby with two of his "exotics" in front of the Carousel Club in downtown Dallas.

The exotic (or stripper) was named Jada, and she was widely known over North Texas for her looks and talents. But I tried to explain to Ruby that we couldn't do an editorial about her just because she had a college education.

"You write a lot of stuff about people that aren't as smart as Jada," he said, "and I think it's only fair the newspaper ought to recognize an exotic that's educated."

I admitted that every editorial page indulged in what was called "Afghanistanism" now and then—offering solutions to situations half a world away while avoiding something at home. But an educated exotic? Well, I just couldn't do it. It took me twenty minutes to persuade him.

Jack Ruby left badly disappointed in both the *Times Herald* and me. But he was polite and even brightened to the point of saying, "Oh, yeah . . . I remember you now. You used to be at the cop shop, didn't you?"

A month or so later I was at a literary party in the old Baker Hotel given Larry McMurtry by the publisher of his new book, *Leaving Cheyenne*. It was a nice-sized gathering and across the room, standing six-foot-five, I saw Edwin (Bud) Shrake, a Dallas sports writer who was also a novelist and spent about as much time on novels as he did on sports. (Years after Bud helped make golf sports history by editing and collaborating with the late Austin golf coach Harvey Penick on the latter's *Little Red Book* and *Little Green Book*. The books became the best-selling sports books ever.)

Bud was with a good looking woman, and he brought her over to where I was, introducing me as "a double-barreled editor: Book Editor *and* Editor of the Editorial Page." The woman smiled politely, unimpressed by my double-barreledness, and Bud said, "A. C., I want you to meet Jada, the star of the Carousel Club," he winked. "She ought to write a book."

Jada ("Jada" was derived from her real name, *Janet Adams Conforto*) was not what I might have expected of an exotic. She was not brassy or slangy—her language was grammatically correct. She used a bit more daytime makeup than was usual, but there was no denying her good looks.

I told Jada that her boss had been up to see me a few weeks before trying to get me to write an editorial about her. She frowned, "An editorial about me? Why in the world would you write an editorial about me?"

"Mr. Ruby said you had a college education, and he thought that was worth a newspaper editorial," I told her.

She let out a laugh. "My god. I attended a little cow college for about one semester—but to Jack that's a college education!"

As demure as Jada appeared at Larry McMurtry's literary gathering, she apparently shed that demeanor when working as a professional. Jack Ruby sometimes shut off the spotlight during her act, accusing her of "going too far" in her stripper routine at the club. Much later, after Ruby and his Carousel Club and Jada (for a while) had become international entities, I reminded Bud Shrake he had told me Jada ought to write a book. I suspect Bud could have made a bestseller of it—and maybe he suspected the same thing.

And sometime or other I lost Jack Ruby's card entitling me to "One free drink at the Carousel Club."

But despite the loss of Lee Harvey Oswald's handwritten letter, and my misplacing Jack Ruby's invitation for a free drink, I came out of that tumultuous period of John F. Kennedy's assassination with a unique reminder of those sad days. It is a black-and-white drawing or sketch of heavy to lighter shaded lines forming an artful picture; a rectangle, diminishing inward to a final small box. The work is very precise, the drawing borders on engineering. I have shown the drawing to dozens of people and have asked them to describe the person who did it, or, the person they imagined would do such a drawing. Nearly everyone has guessed it was done by an orderly, careful person, thinking out the lines of the drawing much the way that person would think out the consequences of any action he or she might take. A psychologist said he thought it indicated a disordered mind, but I suspect the psychologist sensed that guesses were going in the other direction and wanted to display superior mental powers.

The drawing was done by Jack Ruby in his death cell at the Dallas County jail. It is drawn on the back of a 5 x 7 inch jail pass and a domino was used as a straight-edge. Ruby gave it to the *Times Herald* reporter who was on the county beat, Jim (Moonpie) Featherstone. Jim had become something of a confessor for Jack Ruby, going to see him every day and letting Ruby talk his thoughts out. After the drawing was run as artwork for a magazine story (some typical editor wrote "Top" on one of the identical horizontal sides), Jim offered to give the drawing to me but I insisted he take ten dollars. I told him it was worth a great deal more, but he was one of those good-natured, slow talking southerners with his own measurement for the value of things. "Nah, I want you to have it," he said, "You've been pretty fair to Jack and nobody else has." Ruby died of cancer not long after that. By then he'd had access to plenty of editorial pages.

The Midnight General

*I*n 1984, many years after the assassination of President Kennedy, and several years after I had left the daily newspaper business, I wrote a book about Dallas titled *Dallas* USA. Despite having

Edwin Walker

been a Dallas editor during the frantic period before and after the assassination, I tried to write something that showed I had not sacrificed my judgment on the altar of civic defense.

The book, more reportorial than interpretative, came down fairly hard on some Dallas institutions and certain individuals, one of whom was General Edwin Walker. General Walker had been in charge of U. S. Army troops in West Berlin, where he distributed a booklet to his troops pointing out several dangers from the Communists. Washington politicians said the booklet might endanger our Russian diplomacy. Besides, a general had no business messing in political affairs. General Walker returned to the U. S. and quickly became an idol of certain conservative groups.

In my book I reported that after General Walker was fired from command of troops in West Berlin, he was brought to Dallas with Dallas money and entered the 1962 Texas governor's race, which led (I wrote) "to clowning defeat." Later he appeared on the University of Mississippi campus in opposition to James Meredith's enrollment, urging the nation (I said) to grab "a frying pan, a rifle and the flag" and join him. General Walker was hauled off to a government psychiatric center for "study."

I said reporters found it "impossible to make heads or tails of an interview with him unless one of his 'associates' was on hand to inter-pret—to the press *and* to the general." I spoke of his "emotional aberrations" and told of his idiosyncrasies. I spared nothing.

One night in 1986, about 9 o'clock while I was working at home, my wife answered the phone and finally told me on the intercom that "this man" insisted he must talk to me. I told her to put him on, figur-ing it was someone wanting some tidbit of Texas history or a genealo-gist chasing after a great-great grandfather. I wrote (and continue to write) a weekly historical column appearing in *The Dallas Morning News*, so such queries were almost a daily thing. But this was no mere query. When I answered the phone a man's voice said, "This is Edwin Walker. I would like to discuss your book with you."

You can imagine what my feelings were at that instant. General Walker, who had suffered my slings and arrows, as noted, must surely be ready to tear my head off. But no.

"Mr. Greene," he said, "I have just finished reading your book, *Dallas USA*, and I find it very accurate and readable—the best book on Dallas I have read." He paused, and said, "However . . . " and I thought, "Here it comes!" "However," he continued, "there are some errors in what you have written about me that I hope you might want to correct. You seem to want to be accurate."

I assured him that I certainly wanted to hear of any errors I might have made concerning his time in Dallas, and he started on a list.

"First, you said I was fired from command of American troops in West Berlin, but I was not fired. I was relieved of command. And you say that I was 'brought' to Dallas with Dallas money, and that is incor-rect; I returned to Dallas on my own. I bought my home myself. There was no one's money but mine." I had written in 1984 that General Walker no longer lived in Dallas but that, too, was incorrect, he said. "This is still my home."

I was noting his corrections in my copy of the book (which I am reading as I write this) and I felt they were fair. General Walker con-tinued, pointing out that he had not urged the nation to grab a *rifle*, along with the frying pan and the flag. "I suggested a *tent*," he said. He also noted that the government's "kidnapping" (he called it) to take him to a psychiatric ward was illegal, "as ruled by the court." He added that he got a settlement out of the Associated Press when that news organization said, libelously, he had led the Mississippi raid.

I felt a historical necessity to talk with him for as long as he wanted to talk. He related a fascinating account of the attempt to assassinate him in April, 1963, that turned out to have been made by Lee Harvey Oswald. General Walker said he was alone, seated in his study, not realizing he was outlined by a window. "I have had enough experience in wartime that I should have known better than to expose myself so prominently," he said. I agreed that one doesn't suspect that sort of thing in a peacetime Dallas.

He told me that Oswald's bullet hit the double frame of the window and progressed through a plaster wall. It was a near miss. "I found the bullet on the floor, mashed as thin as a quarter," he said. (General Walker had no idea who had fired at him and did not find out it was Lee Harvey Oswald until after Marina Oswald told the nation her husband had come back from the failed attempt and told her for whom it was intended.)

General Walker described to me he next day, how the Federal Bureau of Investigation team that came to check on the shooting would not listen to him at any point, trying to tell him it was one of his crazy followers. In addition, he said, "the bullet the FBI has on display in Washington is not the real bullet. Their bullet is about as long as two joints of your little finger. It is scarcely scratched. I don't know where it came from or why they use it. I have the real bullet that was fired at me and it is flat as a quarter."

General Walker had sold the big gray house in Dallas where he lived for several years after he returned from Germany. Back in the 1960s, we at the *Dallas Times Herald* editorial page had dubbed it "The fortress on Turtle Creek," because the general flew a United States flag in his front yard upside down—the international signal of distress. He told me the distress signal was never intended for Dallas but was for the nation which, he felt, had made some disastrous moves. When General Walker sold The Fortress he took with him that splintered window which Oswald had shot. The new owner threatened a lawsuit, but Walker kept the window.

We talked for at least forty-five minutes that night. General Walker was very considerate, prefacing every correction with an understanding phrase. Of course the old right-wing organizations were long gone from Dallas and Walker himself had been arrested by the Dallas police for "indecent exposure" a couple of times (trapped, some observers felt) and was no longer the fearsome figure of "The Right"— but that was not mentioned. I knew that I was hearing a remarkable recital of history. I wondered that he had been moved to contact me more than two years after the book's publication. There must have been some strong compulsion for him to make those corrections and relate to me the story of how none of the law enforcement authorities, not the Dallas police or even the FBI, took the attempt on his life seriously. He said, only after it was discovered that it was Lee Harvey Oswald who had tried to kill him was any interest shown, and even then people insisted it was insignificant; "maybe he shot at him . . . but he didn't hit him."

A number of writers believed Edwin Walker might have had some connection with the Kennedy assassination. I do not. I think the Kennedy assassination took all the right-wing groups by stunning surprise. General Walker continued to offer anti-communist advice through telephone tapes, but the old militancy of the right-wing was gone, forever. I saw the late General Edwin Walker only once in those days when he was a darling of the far right, and I never heard from him again after that late night telephone call, but I have a kind of pride that he called me. He was looking for a place to deposit history as he saw it. He wanted to be sure. Apparently he thought I was his last resort to get certain things straight. Nobody else would listen. In the next edition of *Dallas USA*, my book was corrected.

When he died a reporter asked me to comment on him. "I understand you interviewed him," the reporter said. "No," I said, "I think he interviewed me."

Chance Encounters
in Love and Fate Along the Way

Young Betty Dozier Greene

(From left to right), A.C., Jerrie Smith,
Fred Smith, and Betty Greene

The Reporter Steals a Wife

As I was preparing for my final year of college, I made a horrible discovery: I needed an additional three hours of advanced English to graduate. I had taken all the advanced hours offered at Abilene Christian College except for Old English, which I feared to take under a capable but daunting Anglo-Saxon called "Hattie"—she who wore a hat while teaching.

I discovered that Hardin-Simmons University, only a couple of miles away, was offering an advance credit Creative Writing course under a visiting author and his wife. It was a night course, meeting once a week, extracting only a modest fee—which Uncle Sam and the G.I. Bill, would pay.

One of my dorm mates named Robert R. Meyers had already braved Hattie's Old English course and didn't need the additional hours, but he had a car and I didn't, so I convinced him he was interested enough in Creative Writing to sign up for the H-SU course with me. (Bob later was professor of English at Wichita University in Kansas, wrote books and numerous magazine articles and became a Congregational minister noted through the midwest.)

Taking the course on a "strange" campus with Bob involved a certain danger for me: social danger. Bob was (and is) a most handsome man, with a god-given ability to attract females, and we were both bachelors. So while neither of us thought primarily in those terms when signing up for this course, I recognized my potential disadvantage if, suddenly, female attraction should become part of the curriculum.

Opening night of the Creative Writing course, Bob and I found ourselves sitting midway up on some risers in a room at H-SU, not a friend or comrade in sight. (Abilene Christian and H-SU had little in common despite having been in the same city for decades.) Suddenly Bob gave me one of those quick nudges that every man understands, and whispered, "Look!"

There were two very pretty girls entering the classroom, and they were being greeted on all sides by male and female alike. When I said to Bob, "Hey, I know that girl on the left. She's Helen Jean Bond. I went to high school with her brother," his face took on a dangerous (to me) glow, and he began laying plans.

At the midway break (this was a three hour class) he and I moved out to where the Coke machine was under siege. The two girls were waiting their turn, and I introduced myself to Helen Jean, told her I remembered her older brother Hall from Abilene High, and made a joking remark about kid sisters who grew up. Bob moved in quickly and took over, once introduced, so I began questioning the other girl. Her name was Betty Dozier, and she was from Dallas. I said, oh good! I was, too. But she wasn't too trusting. "Did you really know Helen Jean's brother?" she challenged. I vowed, Scout's Honor, I did. "Are you actually from Dallas?" she asked, disbelief evident in her question. I vowed this also was true, and she demanded to know where in Dallas I lived.

"I live on Preston Road, along Turtle Creek," I said. This was an attempt to stun her. The location I named is the most exclusive in Dallas, while my real home was miles away. But it is difficult to overwhelm a pretty girl who has been courted, since age fourteen, by a wide range of eligible suitors (airmen, soldiers, Marines, students and veterans). She shrugged off my attempt to pass as a Preston Road millionaire, especially when it turned out I didn't have a nickel (wonderful times!) to buy her a Coke. So she bought me one.

Betty Dozier was well known on the H-SU campus and, I discovered, was going with a handsome football player. Bob and I once offered to take her and Helen Jean out for a hamburger after class, but when they discovered Bob's car had only a front seat—meaning someone would have to ride in someone's lap—they declined. I think Helen Jean might have gone but Betty wouldn't.

Bob performed smoothly in the course, getting well deserved compliments on his writing. I was in a cynical mood that spring, so I became the class reactionary. At one point, after I had written an outrageous story, the instructor announced, "The last time I had a student turn in something like this, he went out and set fire to himself."

Bob and I graduated from Abilene Christian the next year. Bob went back to Oklahoma and married a beautiful blonde sophomore girl named Billie. In the summer of 1948, as mentioned elsewhere, I started to Salida, Colorado, to interview for a teaching job, but stopped in Abilene to have the brakes checked on my 1927 Rolls Royce, and ended up getting a job at the Coca Cola bottling plant where I had worked before the war.

One day I was heading for a cafeteria in downtown Abilene when one of the members of my graduating class, already enrolled in law school, stopped me in the middle of Cypress and North Second streets and stated rather scornfully, "I thought you graduated." I said of course I did. Pointing a finger at the Coca Cola insignia over my shirt pocket he asked sarcastically, "Why?"

Without hesitation, I turned and went across the street to the offices of the *Abilene Reporter-News*, which I had never entered. The Managing Editor's office was on the second floor, and I climbed the stairs, wrestled open the ponderous metal fire door that guarded the news room, and found the M.E.'s office. I told him I wanted to apply for a job. He asked me if I had any newspaper experience, and I said no. He asked me if I had majored in journalism. I told him I had taken only three hours of journalism but it was all a matter of nomenclature anyway. I wanted to be a feature writer. Somehow (still in my Coca Cola uniform) I talked him into letting me write a sample, although there is nothing an M.E. hates worse than someone who announces he or she is a feature writer.

I decided I would write on one of my favorite subjects, the Abilene & Southern Railroad. I went down to the empty passenger station and attempted to buy a ticket. It had been so long since the A&S had sold a full price passenger ticket it took the clerk twenty minutes to find one. I rode the train to the little town of Ballinger and back and wrote a nostalgic story about the trip that made me sound as if I were forty or fifty years old. (I was twenty-four.) When the Managing Editor read it he said, "We don't use first-person features." I figured there was no use pussyfooting, so I said, "Don't worry—you will." He suggested I take the Colorado teaching job, but offered me thirty-five dollars a week to start as a reporter. I took it without a second thought, even though thirty-five dollars was dirt wages, even for common labor.

I had been at work for the newspaper for about three weeks when one day that heavy fire door was pulled opened and a well appointed young woman entered the news room, looked around, and headed for the Woman's Department. I recognized the face. It was my H-SU friend, Betty Dozier. I felt a twinge of jealousy: she was obviously going to the Woman's Department to turn in her wedding announcement. I watched her a while longer and she sat down at a typewriter, which was often the case when brides-to-be wanted to fill out the wedding information sheet on the spot. But after several more minutes she was still there and I thought it was time I show my friendly interest.

I walked over to the Woman's Department and introduced myself and was gratified when Miss Dozier said of course she remembered me. She said she was, as of this date, employed part time by the *Reporter-News* and was in her final year at H-SU. A week or so later I asked if I could take her back to her dorm after work but she thanked me and said someone was picking her up. I envisioned a six-foot-three, sloe-eyed grid hero, but pretended to shrug.

It would be romantic to say shortly after that our various attachments were severed (I was going with a sloe-eyed darling myself), but it was not until the next spring that Miss Dozier and I started dating. After graduation from A.C.C. I roomed with an ex-Navy pilot named Wayne Hefton. He often took me along when he went to Dallas and checked out planes to fly in the Naval Reserve program. One Sunday afternoon when he picked me up to go back to Abilene, he said he had promised a Hardin-Simmons girl he would give her a ride, too. It was Betty. I didn't even know he knew her. Another Navy Reservist, Buzby, was with us on the return trip, and after we had stopped for supper (twenty-five cent hamburgers) Buz begged to stretch out on the back seat and nap. That put me in the front seat with Betty and Wayne, and while going along a rough construction detour, Betty turned and inadvertently hit the headlight switch with her knee, plunging us into darkness. I decided I had waited long enough. I pulled her to me and kissed her. From her response, it was evident we had both been waiting.

So, again, it would be nice to note that shortly after that we became engaged and then proceeded to a lovely church wedding. But that wasn't the case, either. About a year following the headlight incident, we set a Saturday wedding date. We sent out invitations, invited our old friend Bob Meyers to perform the Saturday ceremony, and the day before the wedding—Betty backed out. Bob and the Best Man, also Bob, made their weary way back home.

Monday morning I called her home and said we should talk, but Betty told me she had already made appointments for job interviews in downtown Dallas. I said I would take her. She agreed, with reluctance. When I picked her up she was wearing hose-and-heels and the type dress young lady job applicants favored at the time—plus a hat. We were several miles away from downtown Dallas when she realized the fact, and demanded to know where I thought I was going? I said, evenly, "We are going to Abilene and get married."

She slid as far toward the right-hand car door as possible, and looking straight ahead said, "I will jump out and scream." I warned her that I had a full tank of gas and didn't plan to stop and assured her that at sixty miles-per-hour (my Hudson's top speed) she might find it uncomfortable. To demonstrate my cool, I took out a harmonica (my only instrumental talent) and began playing my limited repertoire. After we had circled Fort Worth and had entered the town of Weatherford she suddenly asked, her first words in fifty miles, "Aren't you even going to buy me breakfast?" I agreed, but she must promise not to create a scene or scream or run off, etc. She shrugged and said, "Don't be silly."

When we were seated in the restaurant and the "hon" waitress ("You want cream, hon? How do you want your eggs, hon?") had taken our order and brought us coffee, Betty looked at me and said, "Let me see my ring." The juke box was playing, "With My Eyes Wide Open I'm Dreaming." We were married that night, May 1, 1950, in

Abilene, the wrong date (April 29) never changed in her wedding ring. The marriage lasted for four kids and thirty-nine years.

A Maine Question, A Texas Answer

*S*everal months after Betty's death, I was visiting Dallas friends, Fred and Jerrie Smith at their summer home in West Rockport, Maine. As was nearly always the case with Smith summers, visitors came and went—or stayed—at a great pace. To spend time at the Smiths' Maine home is more than pleasant, and you are reluctant to end your stay; the company is always dear and the surroundings are exceptionally beautiful. In fact, from most rooms of the house anyone with some literary memory may suddenly realize he or she is looking at the opening verse of Edna St. Vincent Millay's early poem, "Renascence":

> *All I could see from where I stood*
> *Was three long mountains and a wood.*
> *I turned and looked the other way*
> *And saw three islands in a bay.*

The first time I had stepped out on a Smith balcony and looked around, the verse automatically occurred to me. I didn't find out until later that Edna St. Vincent had lived in nearby Camden, and what I saw was literally the view which inspired that verse.

At any rate, as enjoyable as was the time in Maine, it was at the end of a sad summer for me, the spring death of Betty taking out all other thoughts for the time. I had been invited to a couple of dinners given by Dallas friends, but I felt only half of me was there. I had been to New York to discuss my book *Taking Heart* with my editor, and despite a satisfactory literary outcome, the trip was lonely. I was in Maine for spiritual resuscitation, not social recreation.

Fred Smith and I were sitting on the patio having drinks one afternoon and Fred said, in his Maine native's accent, "Now, A. C., you know, we all loved Betty, but she has been gone for some time now . . . are you going out among the ladies again?"

The phrase had a foreign sound: "out among the ladies." Old fashioned phrase, but also unfamiliar, like dating, after thirty-nine years of marriage. In my mind the answer was, no. I wasn't ready to go "out among the ladies." I hadn't thought about it, didn't want to think about it. In the first place, I felt I was too old to be dating—the very word embarrassed me—and I couldn't see myself paying court to some female stranger, no matter how young or attractive she might be.

But then I admitted, to myself, that loneliness was the occupational hazard of the widower, used to the comfort of always having a confidante, a loving helpmeet, as the Bible puts it. I missed love, not just physical love, but having someone near me toward whom I felt the

A.C. and Judy Greene. The stagecoach is in Salado, our home town.

kind of affection that comes from shared experience, from similar thoughts, aims and joined lives. Could this ever be regained?

Then, inspired by Fred's chance remark, I recalled someone, a friend I hadn't seen in two or three years, and the last time I had seen her she was being escorted by a handsome millionaire. I hesitated for a moment, then said, "Well, yes . . . I may do that." (I couldn't bring myself to say I may be "going out among the ladies.")

"Do you have anyone in mind?" Fred asked, and (although I hadn't had anyone in mind a few seconds ago) I said, "Yes. Judy Hyland."

Fred, said, "Oh, excellent choice. Fine lady."

When I returned to Dallas I was undecided about what to do. I had given little or no thought to a new romance, but once expressed, the idea of seeing Judy again held more and more appeal. She and her first husband had been close friends with Betty and me, but after they divorced several years earlier, I only saw Judy at friends' parties a few times each year. Judy had gone back to school and gotten an advanced degree and had held some high-level professional positions, which gradually removed her from our little married group, and for two or three years I was out of the loop myself with my bad heart. Judy had written numerous notes to me about my heart condition, and after Betty's death had sent me a letter explaining her own mother had been dying in Missouri at the time of Betty's funeral, but I wasn't sure Judy was still single—or uncommitted. In addition, Judy was a decade or so younger than I, and very attractive. Trying to win her would be a gamble, with long odds, but I decided I wanted to make it.

I called Ann, a mutual friend, and asked about Judy in as casual a way as possible. Ann told me Judy was not married but had retired from her last position and was moving to California where her older daughter had just presented Judy with her first grandchild, a little girl named for her. Ann gave me Judy's unlisted phone number but when I called it I was told the number was no longer in service. Did this mean Judy had already made the westward move? After several more tries, always getting the same automated answer, I called Ann back and told her of my predicament. "Oh, dear," she sighed, "I guess I gave you her old number. I forgot she has a new one. Let me see if I can find it."

By now tracking down Judy had become a challenge. Ann finally uncovered the new number and when I tried it I at least got Judy's answering machine. I left a message that I would like to hear from her; nothing romantical or hinting at things romantical. Then I waited and waited; left other messages on the machine—and waited some more. Finally I got a reply. Judy called, saying she had been in California. I asked her if she was going to move there and she said she planned to "as soon as I sell my townhouse." I asked her to go to a garden party with me, and she agreed. I found myself as excited as a high school boy at his first prom. Then, the day of the big outdoor function, the heavens opened as only the heavens can open in Texas, and the floods descended—and the party was washed out.

Judy was unable to find an open date immediately: she was going to Lubbock one week end, to Oklahoma City the next. I persisted, knowing I had to beat her California deadline. I finally pinned down a time and said I would take her to Mario Leal's Chiquita, a Mexican food place we both liked. After getting lost twice (nervous?), I found her townhouse and Judy and I talked for an hour, catching up on our lives, before we went to the restaurant.

We walked into Chiquita, and the first person we saw was Fred Smith, my Maine host. He took for granted things had already been set up with Judy when I was in Maine. He didn't realize his chance question had started the whole process.

Judy and I were married some months after that—and several wonderful years ago.

The Steam-Piano Player

The summer of 1955, when I owned a book store in Abilene, I stepped out of my little shop and was suddenly blasted by a wailing sound like a thousand bagpipes. It seemed to originate along the Wichita Valley railroad tracks. Was this the cry of a steam locomotive in its death throes?

Telling my young female assistant I would be back as soon as I discovered what was making the frightening noise, I took off in pursuit of the sound, which was progressing down Pine, the city's main business street. When I caught up with "it" I saw "it" was a steam calliope and the "noise" was actually music . . . sort of.

This calliope was pulled by a tractor and was larger than what I could recall of circus calliopes. It was painted a bright red and gold, and given to steam hissings at all times, the way a steam locomotive pants steam even when it's not moving.

I joined the crowd following the calliope's parade, which included flag-bearing riders straight off the range, a stagecoach, a chuckwagon, and lovely ladies expertly riding side-saddle. I realized this was the announcement parade for the annual *Fort Griffin Fandangle*, the famed outdoor spectacle from Albany, Texas, a small town a few miles north of Abilene.

The *Fandangle*, I knew, was completely home-grown: the actors and singers were all from Shackleford County, of which Albany is the county seat, and the music and theatrical segments were written by

Bob Green

homemade talent. I reasoned the calliope must be homemade, too, as must the player.

I was doubly correct. The calliope had been constructed in Albany by J. P. Crutchfield's welders and metal workers, built of various pipes and metals from oil field salvage. And for this, the calliope's first public concert, I recognized the man at the keyboard as one of my book customers, a rancher named Bob Green—or James Robert, if more formality is required. Bob, who had acted in the very first *Fandangle* as a high school student, was a narrator for the *Fandangle* as well as the player of the calliope.

Two years later when I was out of the book business and back in the newspaper business, I spent two days doing a series of stories about how the *Fandangle* was put together, helpfully guided by the late Robert Nail, producer and originator of the *Fandangle*. Of course, the first person I met was the *Fandangle's* calliope player, Bob Green. It didn't take but a few sentences for us to start remembering incidents in my bookstore. As Bob Green and I turned out to be about the same age and have about the same name, mutually loved history, books and music, our friendship was instant and seemingly predestined—we were both Presbyterians, too. And later I was to find the calliope was just the most exotic instrument Bob Green played, not the only one. He also played piano, electronic organ, accordian, mouth organ, guitar and probably a couple of others. Forty-four years later, I still haven't exhausted Bob's musical talents.

Bob Nail took me out to the Green Ranch the next night, where the Greens had invited us for swimming and picnicking at their big pond, or tank, that was fitted with dock and float for swimming, with tables and chairs for eating. After the picnic, while Bob Nail was teaching dance steps to Nancy Green and daughter Nancy Kate, Bob Green and I talked history. I came away from that evening on the ranch with a friendship which has never faltered in the nearly five decades since: Bob Green, we all realize, is the kind of a man that God only made one of.

Former board member of the Albany National Bank, active in all kinds of civic undertaking, from Albany High School football games to the nationally famed Old Jail Art Center, to the restored Fort Griffin State Park, Bob is a participant in his support, not just a contributor. He has written a weekly newspaper column, contributed to several books, and always makes the more important speeches in Shackleford County celebrations. On the other hand, Bob Green has traveled extensively, usually in pursuit of some historical or cultural point in Europe—or to places like Iceland and Scotland in pursuit of salmon. His wartime experiences gave him a wide exposure to the South Pacific, the Philippines and Okinawa. He has traveled all over the west on business and has visited most of the battle sites of the Civil War, taking not just a Southerner's point of view but with an open use of history. He has had, at the ranch, several famous historians of various concepts, one or two who didn't know as much about the subject as Bob, but he never indulges in raucous debate. He is also an impartial political observer. Once, in Washington, escorting a piece of sculpture from the Old Jail Art Center for a Rose Garden exhibit, on meeting Hillary Clinton (whose husband he had not voted for), Bob said gallantly and sincerely, "You're a lot prettier than your pictures."

During their father's life, Bob, his two brothers and their sister, were part of the Green Land and Cattle Co., an enterprise which went back to 1888 with land in several locations in the West. Bob's father, Henry Green, a new graduate of Tehuacana College (now Trinity University), had come out to the Shackelford area to sell a herd of free-range horses for his dad, but he was so impressed by the grass and water of Hubbard Creek valley he decided to stay. He bought land with the horse sale money instead of taking it back to his father. After a train trip to Albany by the irate father to see where his money had gone, he had to agree it seemed like a fair investment, but as Henry, the son, took his father back to the train, the father gave him a fifty dollar gold piece and said, "When this runs out, you sell the land and come on back home." That was in 1888, and the fifty dollar gold piece, never spent, is still in the Green family. Bob's ranch includes most of the original acreage. (Henry Green died in 1952 at age eighty-four in an auto accident.)

The Green families are historically and emotionally tied to the town and the country around Albany. Albany is not a deserted relic from the frontier nor is it an artificially preserved exhibit—it is a vigorous modern town. It has two restored theaters and an acclaimed art museum. The town delights in living with a historic past that Bob Green and his kind have helped document and save. Bob was one of three writers who helped produce a historical volume in 2001 honoring the newly renovated 1883 Shackleford County courthouse that is the center of much community life and love.

But Bob Green is more than a West Texas rancher and a historian. He is a pantheist. His pantheon is his earth and everything that walks and crawls across it or flies above it. Or has, in the past, used or visited it. Taking a tour of his ranch in a bouncing pickup is a period of worship, with Bob as priest. It is where he was born, where he was raised, where he became a cowboy and a rancher, a husband, father and philosopher—and where he will be buried. Despite the size of his home place, some thirty sections, there is scarcely a rock or a tree Bob doesn't have direct association with. And as for the animals, beyond the cattle and horses that are an understood part of a West Texas ranch, he protects the natural denizens like children—the land's children and his own. As we drove through a pasture, one cloudy afternoon, he pointed to a wooded hillock, rising on the south. "That's where the coyotes live. I call them the Hill Tribe." I asked how long the animals had nested at that site and he grinned, "Oh, I guess for a thousand years. They were there a good bit before the Greens came on the place." Doesn't he find it dangerous to run cattle and coyotes on the same ranch? "Not so far—" and we can surmise the Hill Tribe will be safe as long as Bob Green is around.

Nancy Green, a Houston beauty who had never been on a ranch until she married Bob, has never opposed Bob's care for the ranch wildlife, but she was once heard to tell a visitor, "Oh, we're not raising cattle any more. We're raising deer." As if to back up her statement, that particular visitor in one large pasture was able to count in excess of 300 deer. Driving toward Hubbard Creek Lake, which borders the eastern side of the J. R. Green ranch (and which submerged old Henry Green's original homestead when it was built in 1962), we see an equal number of wild turkeys, among the shyest of wild game. It is no trouble to spot a big tom leading his family along at a dignified trot. Antelope may be glimpsed, too, and for years Bob allowed no hunting except for some fall dove and quail shooting by friends, but by the turn of the new century, Bob, almost by ecological necessity, leased 10,000 acres to a group of sportsmen (chosen by son Rob, a prominent Fort Worth lawyer). The hunters erected a semi-village of trailer homes, with a big cold vault, separate electrical service and a separate ranch entrance.

A modern ranch must raise cattle that will market best, and the days of only beautiful blocky Herefords are pretty well past. Herefords are Bob's favorite breed, but he now raises crossbreds, utilizing Charolais, Simmentals and Black and Red Angus or old-timey Texas Longhorn bulls for breeding, producing a faster maturing, bigger animal with more of the kind of meat America now buys—fewer prime steaks but more pounds of salable beef.

Wild hogs and boars are always on the scene (sows give birth to ten to eleven piglets at a time), although due to government packing regulations they can't be marketed. The wild hogs are probably descended from hogs introduced to West Texas by nineteenth century English ranch owners who enjoyed the sport of "pig sticking." The cowboys, with Bob's okay, sometimes trap hogs for personal consumption.

Bob raises his own feed and hay and has built several sizable tanks, or ponds—and in addition to the earthmovers the contractors use, Bob has a fleet of trucks and bulldozers and graders. And all these tractors, balers, and pickups call for someone at the wheel—not to mention someone doing such traditional jobs as grubbing out cactus and stringing fence, or laying irrigation pipe.

The cook shack, with a complete professional kitchen, is where cook Roberto keeps breakfast and lunch ready to be served to anywhere from six to two dozen "drop-ins." The cook shack is part of the complex of home for Roberto and family, which includes huge feed bins, tractor and equipment sheds, pens for horses—and home range for a dozen busy cats.

I am a city person, but nothing can compare to the distant vistas, the sounds, the smells, the sights of truly open country—the grass, whether green or brown, going off in waves at the slightest touch of the wind, the clouds moving in shadows cast right at your feet, wedges of Canadian honkers in season, the swing of hawks and vultures, one pond where a dozen dead trees are festooned with the ragged nests of cranes, the cries of scissor-tailed flycatchers, field larks, mockingbirds, killdeers, the coo of doves in the early morning or the hoot of owls at dusk along the creeks, the yip-yap of coyotes at night. And to experience such country with someone who, as he says, temporarily owns it, but regards it as part of all humanity, is inspiring. Bob is an environmentalist and an ecologist, but from the rare end: actually possessing and operating the environment and the ecology he aspires to protect.

Bob's favorite animal, if that's the word, is the old box turtle, the dry land terrapin. It pains him that some of the people he employs on the ranch (and operating a ranch is a major business involving all kinds of people) run over them with cars or trucks. Or, take snakes. Only reluctantly will Bob kill a rattlesnake, and then it will have to be too near a house or barn. One doesn't have to go exploring to find skunks, armadillos, porcupines or rabbits on the ranch. I cited the supposed danger of multiplying rabbits taking over, but Bob laughs, "With the coyotes and bobcats to keep down the varmint population, the balance is pretty well maintained." Now and then, he admits, the coyotes may kill a new calf or an injured deer—it's rare—but even then, the coyotes are worth the loss.

But the land itself, not its animal population alone, is what Bob Green loves so innately that he suffers with it in drouth and rejoices in rain. But like a venerable West Texas joke implies, an experienced rancher is pessimistic. The story tells of an old rancher who is with a friend watching a downpour. The friend turns to the rancher and says, "Well, this will take care of rainfall for this year," but the old rancher shook his head sadly. "This here's exactly how the last drouth started."

One evening, as he entertained a group of us by playing the accordion on the patio at the ranch house, Bob folded his musical box and ran into the front yard half a dozen times to get a better view of the weather. What he wanted was a good hard "turd floater" rain to fill the ranch tanks and ponds, and from the accumulation of heavy clouds and the thunder and lightning, I would have bet good money that a young flood would descend on the ranch at any moment, but Bob was pessimistic. "No, it's going to miss us," he assured a visiting neighboring landowner. When a mild sprinkle set up, I yelled in delight that Bob had been wrong, but he persisted in pessimism, and he was right. The sprinkle turned into fitful spit. "Well, that'll help the grass," he consoled himself.

One time, some years ago, Bob told me the working cowboy was a vanishing species, but later he introduced me to Bennie Peacock, whom he called "A real cowboy." He worked for Bob as a ranch manager for many years. The first time I met Bennie, he and Bob talked a variety of ranch subjects that would have bewildered a traditional cowboy—about irrigation pumps cycling, boring and filling holes with concrete off a transit mix truck, and how many acres of oats should have been baled by 5 P.M. Bennie looks like a country and western music idol, but that undefinable love of land, of animals, of life alone and in the open, shines on his face and in his conversation.

Bob in person fits the popular image of a Texas rancher—old Stetson, worn boots, khaki pants and work shirt—but behind the feed-truck steering wheel is a natural philosopher. Bob is a graduate of the University of Texas at Austin, where he met Nancy Ebersole, of Houston, and won her hand by enrolling in some of her classes, including cooking.

His spacious home, which began as an 1894 line camp, contains an outstanding library, particularly World War II histories and rare Texana, and his role as a regional historian is substantial. He can (and does) talk literature knowledgeably with the Irish, the English—or Texans. He was a pilot for years and has had five planes for use in cattle buying—and history. He and I once flew the Butterfield Trail across Texas in preparation for a book I was to write. When published, I dedicated the book in the best way I could express my personal love and feeling for him: "To Bob Green—Brother, not of blood but of spirit."

Bob was a tank commander during World War II and won the Silver Star for bravery on Okinawa saving his tank crew by exposing himself to constant enemy fire as he opened the escape hatch for his crew to flee their stricken tank. He went into the Army from New Mexico Military Institute (Paul Horgan was one of his teachers) and was commissioned second lieutenant at age nineteen.

Until one of those coast-to-coast robbery gangs pulled a moving van to his back door and cleaned him out, some time ago, he had one of the best flint and stone implement collections in the United States, a lot of it found on his ranch. As you would expect, he is a sure quail shot and, until age warned him against it, a fine horseman, which he became at age three. His favorite mount, that he kept long after he quit riding, died at age thirty.

Despite his enthusiasm for his way of life, Bob admits that today, it might be almost impossible to operate any large Texas ranch solely on cattle. The economics of meat marketing are in favor of the cattle buyer, not the seller. Cattle prices have steadily declined—not to mention fanatical attempts to eliminate "red meat" from the national diet.

Several thousand of Bob's acres touch Hubbard Creek Lake, and could be sold at premium prices, and his entire ranch is an outstanding example of land care and use. In other words, if ranching became unbearably uneconomical, there are potential millions to be made from sale of his ranch land.

But saying it—possibly even thinking it—brings fierce reaction from Bob Green. "I guess I ought to think about it, maybe I ought to do it. But I can't sell this land. It's me."

★ ★ ★

And situated atop a knoll, under clumps of oak, looking down a long valley, is a part of the J. R. Green ranch that is mine. Not only were Judy and I married in 1990 in front of Bob's big fireplace, purposely constructed "big enough to roast an ox," but we spent our wedding night at the Lake House, on Hubbard Creek Lake, arriving there late after Nancy Green's big party in our honor. Judy and I sat wrapped in bliss on the verandah of the Lake House until the early morning hours, listening to the coyotes yip-yipping like a thousand voices all across the horizon.

On that knoll that is my part of the ranch, is buried Betty, my late wife of thirty-nine years, at home on the ranch she loved. And if life works out as planned, someday she will be joined by Judy and me, united in the Green Family cemetery along with Bob and Nancy and many other Green family and Albany friends.

Index

Photo Credits

The sources for the photographs in this book appear below.
Credits from left to right are separated by semicolons.

Dustjacket: Photo by Bill Wittliff

3: The collection of A. C. Greene

5: The collection of A. C. Greene

6: The collection of A. C. Greene; ©Bettman/CORBIS

13: ©Bettman/CORBIS

14: The collection of A. C. Greene

19: ©Bettman/CORBIS

22: ©Bettman/CORBIS

25: The collection of A. C. Greene

27: Photo by A. C. Greene

29: The collection of A. C. Greene; The collection of A. C. Greene

39: ©Bettman/CORBIS

40: The collection of A. C. Greene; Photo by A. C. Greene

47: Photo courtesy of Mrs. Jack McGuire

51: ©Bettman/CORBIS

52: ©Wally McNames/CORBIS

62: Courtesy of Bob Daemmrich Photo Inc.

65: Official White House photo

67: ©Bettman/CORBIS

68: ©Hulton-Deutsch Collection/CORBIS

78: ©Bettman/CORBIS

82: Courtesy of the *Dallas Morning News*

86: ©Bettman/CORBIS

94: ©Hulton-Deutsch Collection/CORBIS

97: Courtesy of the University of North Texas Library Archives

101: ©Bettman/CORBIS

107: Family photo

111: ©Bettman/CORBIS

114: ©Bettman/CORBIS

115: ©Hulton-Deutsch Collection/CORBIS

117: ©Bettman/CORBIS

118: ©James L. Amos/CORBIS

120: ©Hulton-Deutsch Collection/CORBIS

123: ©Joseph Lederer/CORBIS OUTLINE

130: ©Bettman/CORBIS

133: Courtesy of Artie Shaw

134: The collection of A. C. Greene

138: ©Bettman/CORBIS

141: Courtesy of Stanley Marcus

143: ©Ted Streshinsky/CORBIS; Courtesy of the Texas Folklore Society

145: ©Bettman/CORBIS

148: Courtesy of the *Dallas Morning News*

149: Courtesy of the *Dallas Morning News*; The collection of A. C. Greene

151: Courtesy of the *Dallas Morning News*

153: ©Bettman/CORBIS

161: ©CORBIS

162: Courtesy of the *Dallas Morning News*

165: Courtesy of the *Dallas Morning News*

168: ©Bettman/CORBIS

171: ©CORBIS

187: The collection of A. C. Greene

188: The collection of A. C. Greene

195: The collection of A. C. Greene

198: The collection of A. C. Greene

The defining nature of a chance encounter is unexpe